Smart Pickleball™

The Pickleball Guru's Guide

By Prem Carnot
with Wendy Garrido

Feedback on this book...

"Many have found Prem's clinics to be a life-changing experience. I've taken his clinic and I've read this book. It is truly a virtual replication of his clinics. By implementing the 'secrets' found here, you'll raise your pickleball game to a level of which you only once dreamed."

— Linda Scott | USAPA District Ambassador

"This book is one of a kind. It's the first real 'How To' pickleball book! It talks about getting results—not learning someone else's technique and it doesn't tell you to hit a shot without breaking that shot down into bite-size pieces. This book works hard to make you...yes...a **smarter** *pickleball player."*

— A.J. Fraties | Palm Creek PB Club, Casa Grande, AZ

"This will be a book I come back to time and again. The lessons from Prem's **Smart Pickleball** *will stick with me and better my game! Just as taking one of Prem's clinics has stuck with me and bettered my game—not all at once but it is knowledge that grows and I treasure it each time I play pickleball."*

— Carol Amos | USAPA Facebook Ambassador

"Through dialogue with the reader, Prem gets us to see that there should be a purpose to each hit other than simply returning the ball. Playing 'smart' is a whole different game from just hitting the ball and moving around the court."

— John Croes | Melbourne, FL

Published by
The Pickleball Guru

First Edition

International Standard Book Number:
ISBN-13: 978-1502596024
ISBN-10: 1502596024

Book and Cover Design by Wendy Garrido

Dedication

To my students and teachers, both past and future, all along the way.

Acknowledgments

As I sit to write this piece my thoughts go down memory lane, thinking of all the people I've met, chatted with, picked their brains, and shared some hearty pickleball moments. It feels a little daunting to name all of those wonderful people who have impacted my life. So I will start by saying thank you from the bottom of my heart to those unnamed who have been part of my pickleball journey.

Here, I will try to mention some individuals who have had a particularly powerful impact on my pickleball journey.

First and foremost to my wife, Wendy, for being the love, the mother and my partner (in pickleball and in life), and for her constant support in every domain of my life. I give her ninety percent of the credit for bringing my teaching into the written world, both online and in this book. She is the woman behind everything. Thank you, sweetie.

To Sue Woodward for always being my business manager, my biggest advocate, and for your unbridled creativity and trust. You keep pushing me to excel. Thank you for the confidence.

To Ron Beachy, the man who relentlessly goaded me into learning this crazy game and later invited me to Nationals.

To Jim Schiller, for pushing me to step into my purpose as a coach and for coining the name "The Pickleball Guru."

To Lethia Owens for the encouragement and prodding that helped me make the mindset shift from being a reluctant coach to developing a flourishing business.

To my father-in-law, Don Garrido, for his unwavering support of our entrepreneurial endeavors.

To my buddy, Billy Jacobsen, for being a friend, supporter, someone I could share my thoughts with and who always makes me laugh.

To Kevin Curley for being a committed member of Team Guru.

And, to Cliff Pelloni for being the promotional guru behind this book.

Table of Contents

Foreword

I met Prem Carnot and his lovely wife Wendy six years ago at the very first ever Open Nationals in Surprise, Arizona. We chatted for a while and discovered we lived about two hours from each other in Washington state. We made arrangements to visit him at his home.

It wasn't long until we both realized our mutual love for racket sports in general and pickleball in particular. Since I'm deaf and can't converse on the phone, I was excited to discover that Prem was someone who would set aside the time to read and write extended emails. Over the years, we have become really good email buddies, talking sports, life, relationships, and countless jokes.

We often meet up at pickleball tournaments and Prem always has a keen observation or very interesting point to make. He has a really good eye and feel for what is happening during a pickleball match.

Over the years he has developed the ability to watch and observe your game and to instantly tell you what you can do to get better. Since Prem has an easy-going, laid back personality and is always smiling, people are easily drawn to him, which makes him an especially good fit for coaching.

Since he decided to become a full-time pickleball coach two years ago, he travels the country giving clinics everywhere. From these clinics Prem has learned a ton about coaching and about how people think when they are playing the game of pickleball. Hence he has written this book.

I really enjoyed reading *Smart Pickleball* and there is lots to learn from it. Use Prem's book to learn from and add to your game. Sometimes one tiny bit of information can change your game like magic for the better. I'm sure every player, from beginner to advanced, will find something in Prem's book to greatly improve your game. After all, isn't continuous improvement what life (and pickleball) is all about?

Sincerely,
Billy Jacobsen

Billy Jacobsen has been playing Open level pickleball tournaments for 33 years. He has won over 70 Open Singles tournaments and 60 Open Doubles events. He has won Gold Medals in both Singles and Doubles in the US National tournament as well as the Canadian Nationals. He lives in Lake Tapps, Washington.

Introduction

Why I Wrote This Book & How You Can Make the Most of It

I wrote this book in response to the many requests (and a few demands!) that I put down in writing all the tips, strategies, drills and information that I share in my Pickleball Guru Academy clinics. People asked to be able to take it all home to read, review, and practice.

For nearly two years I have published a monthly email newsletter (you can subscribe by going to my website, www.ThePickleballGuru.com) where I share articles and blog posts about pickleball strategy and etiquette.

This book includes nearly all the articles published on my website, as well as most of the information I share in my introductory clinics, and more.

So why am I giving you practically ALL of my secrets right here?

Here's why…

Why I'm Giving Away Virtually All My Secrets

There will be a few of you (admittedly, the minority) who will devour every single page of this book, and then get a buddy and start putting into practice every recommendation in this book, chapter by chapter, drill by drill.

You are the "appliers." You're the players who *inspired* me to share every single secret. You know when you've found a good thing, you're committed to improving your game, and you know that just reading about what to do isn't going to be enough. You know you've got to practice, practice, practice.

My secrets are for you.

On the other hand, the majority of readers will most likely read this book, maybe take a few notes, and walk away with one or two learnings that they'll *try* to implement next time they're on the court—*if* they remember (and considering some people's memory issues, that's a big if!) ☺

They are the "forgetters."

The forgetters are the players who led me to decide that it really doesn't *matter* if I share every single secret, because the majority of what I share will go in ear and out the other. (Or is it in one eye and out the other for a book?)

Now, I don't mean to be pessimistic, and I have certainly skimmed through my fair share of books on other topics, picking up some pointers and then promptly forgetting most of it. But if you really do want to play Smart Pickleball™, I'd like to challenge you to not just *read* the information in this book, but come up with a plan to start *applying* it.

If you're serious about playing better and winning more, you can't be a forgetter. You've got to be an applier. The information in this book must not only make it into your long-term memory, but even more importantly, into your *muscle* memory. And *that* takes practice.

It's just the way it is.

Let me be clear. If you just wanna go out, get some exercise and have a blast, you're absolutely 100% entitled to do that without ever practicing a shot.

But if you're set on improving your level of play, you *have to* practice to get better. You *have to* play against different players to get better. You *have to* pay for your mistakes in order to get better.

You *won't* get better if you keep doing the exact same things you've always done. You *won't* win more games if you keep making the same number of unforced errors. And, you can wish all you want that the tooth-fairy will grant you better pickleball skills, but I regret to say, it probably isn't going to help you the next time you're out on the court.

Ask Yourself, "How Could I Do This Better or More Consistently?"

So I invite you to come into this book with a beginner's mind. If you really want to improve your game, be willing to stop saying, "I already know that," and start asking, "How could I do this better or more consistently?"

Are you ready to put in the time and energy to improve? Are you ready to take advantage of every opportunity that comes your way?

Then start practicing.

What to Expect

This book is full of secrets and strategies that will give you better results—without having to beef up, speed up or go back in time—whether you're a new pickleball lover or a long-time pickleball addict.

It focuses on doubles strategy since the majority of players only play doubles, and because it's in doubles play where the unique constraints of pickleball really make a difference.

This book is not intended to teach the rules of pickleball to someone who has never played before. (There are plenty of great resources online and a few other books that can teach you that.)

It's also not intended to teach you a one-size-fits-all solution for how to hit a shot. I don't believe in one-size-fits-all teaching.

(I always like to say that you can take the top ten players on the national pickleball circuit and you'll see ten different ways to hold a paddle or hit a serve, depending on whether they have a background in tennis, table tennis, badminton, or no racket sport experience at all.)

My goal as a teacher is to help you play *YOUR* game better. In fact, the success of my clinics is in large part because I *don't* teach anyone to rebuild their shots from scratch according to *my* idea of how they should play.

Here's some feedback I got from one student (now a good buddy) who ordered a video analysis.

> *"I am very impressed. Where others tend to coach based on their perceptions of how the game should be played by all, your observations were particular to the things I do, both good and bad....*
>
> *I feel much more confident now – I know what I have to work on, and, perhaps more importantly, I know how to work on these things."*
>
> — A.J. Fraties | Casa Grande, AZ

With this book, my purpose is to offer you more efficient and effective ways of playing *your* game. If you want to try out some different ways of holding your paddle, there are plenty of pickleball teachers and tennis coaches who can show you a variety of grips—and will probably also tell you which one *they* think you should use.

My focus is on helping you achieve the successful *outcomes* you're looking for, no matter what style, habits or methodology you already have in place.

Learning to Play Smart Pickleball™ is an Implicit Process

You can relate learning how to play Smart Pickleball™ to learning how to ride a bike.

If I were teaching you to ride a bike, my job would be to make sure you understand the goal (to move forward in an upright position without your feet touching the ground) and to create a safe environment for you to practice. It's your brain's job, through trial and error, to figure out exactly what it needs to do for you to ride a bike. It's *not* my job to push your legs down for you or take a measurement so you know exactly how hard I push down on the pedals so you can copy me.

Just like learning to walk, talk, ride a bike or drive a car, learning to play Smart Pickleball™ is what scientists call an *implicit* learning process. This means that although we can learn HOW to do it, we don't have the conscious understanding to explain WHAT we know.

You can *logically* explain to someone how to figure out what the score is, but can you logically explain how to hit a drop shot? And even if you could, would another person be able to figure it out *simply* by following your instructions?

No, because learning to hit a good drop shot is an *implicit* process. It is something that our brain has to figure out *for* us — it's not something we can just follow a recipe for in order to get the correct solution.

Contrary to what some of you jokesters might think, the alternative—*explicit* learning—has nothing to do with anything R-rated. *::wink, wink::* An example of *explicit* learning is how we learn to keep score in pickleball, or how we know whose turn it is to serve (most of the time we do, anyway). It's just a matter of memorizing a set of rules like following a recipe.

So if learning to hit good shots in pickleball ISN'T something you can learn consciously, then how the heck are you supposed to get better?

That's why practice is truly so important.

The definition of practice is: attempting it often enough that your brain finally figures out how to do it right on purpose.

After all, it's not as if some fairy godmother came and waved a wand and suddenly you could drive a car *and* shift gears *while* making a left-hand turn *with* the radio on *while* talking to your honey in the other seat, right? You mastered that skill through PRACTICE.

You tried it enough times that your brain figured out—*implicitly*—what it needed to do, even though you can't consciously explain how you can estimate the speed of the oncoming traffic in order to know when it's safe to turn—you just KNOW.

You probably had to fall over on a bike twenty-five times before you finally figured out how to ride it, and then how did you know how to do it? You just KNEW.

But, most of us have forgotten what it takes to just *know* how to do something. Think about a child learning to walk. Kids naturally depend on their capacity to learn. They know innately that they are making progress through those twenty five failed attempts and are content to keep trying 'til they get it right.

On the other hand, those of us in the double digits tend to focus on the fact that we "just keep failing" and get frustrated and impatient, wondering what's wrong with us that we haven't gotten it right yet.

If playing pickleball was just a matter of following the recipe, you'd be a 5.0 player in no time because you would just decide to follow the steps and get there.

Because it's an *implicit* learning process, we can't just decide what we want and follow the steps. *Yes*, you MUST know what you want, but then you have to give your brain enough time and repetition to build the neuropathways—after all, that's what learning is.

Occasionally, you may need an outside perspective on the mechanics of your shot, but more often than not, when you know what you're trying to do and you put in time to practice and experiment, your brain will figure out exactly what it needs for you to get the result you want.

What I Mean by Smart Pickleball™

I'll delve into the following principles more in the rest of the book, but here's a quick overview of what I consider to be the rules of playing Smart Pickleball.™

Smart Pickleball™ is about strategically setting yourself up to win a point by biding your time, using your energy efficiently, playing the percentages and anticipating several shots ahead.

The Rules of Smart Pickleball™

1. Always choose the shot that buys you more time so you can get into position and be ready for the next shot.

2. Always choose the shot that keeps your opponents toward the back of the court.

3. Always choose the shot or strategy that requires the least energy or effort to play out the point.

4. Always play the higher-percentage shot.

5. Always anticipate your next shot as you play your current shot.

Smart Pickleball™ is about taking control of the game and constructing each point so that you're not mindlessly reacting to every shot.

I'll go into more depth throughout the rest of this book. For now, read this quote from one of my students and consider yourself enrolled in a virtual version of my introductory Pickleball Guru Academy clinic.

Class is about to begin...

"Just wanted to thank you Prem for the excellent clinic held this week at Hilton Head, South Carolina. I wasn't sure what to expect when I heard you were coming to town, but I signed up for your clinic and the small group lesson. Both were excellent - and I have completely changed how I play the game.

Prem, you not only told us WHAT to do, but you explained WHY what you were telling us made sense to playing better pickleball. I can't wait to practice what I have learned so I can improve."

—Wade Johnson | Hilton Head, SC

Welcome to the Pickleball Guru Academy - Day 1: How to Win a Point in the First Three Shots

Welcome

Now, I want you to imagine that the local pickleball ambassador in your area has organized a Pickleball Guru Academy clinic at your favorite venue.

We've got about fifty players gathered around one of the courts. They are sitting on the bleachers, or chairs they've brought, and I'm standing in front of the group.

The title of the first day's clinic is "How to Win a Point in the First Three Shots."

I start off the day with a brief welcome and introduction.

I explain that I'm a French citizen who grew up in India and moved back to France in my late teens, where I joined a table-tennis club and ended up winning the silver medal in the French national tournament in 1992. (Incidentally, the guy who I eventually lost to went on to win the world championship the next year and was one of the first players in the sport to make millions.)

After that tournament, I was offered a chance to play professionally. At that time, there wasn't a lot of money to be made in table tennis (it was only a little better known back then than pickleball is now).

As I considered my options, I remembered a time as a young teen, when I wanted to play big-time cricket back in India. My dad's words rang in my head, *Sports won't feed you, degrees will. You can't make money as an athlete...It's not a respectable profession...* So I opted to continue down the safer, more traditional route of hotel management.

And, luckily I did, because I met my wife, Wendy, back in 2000 when I was managing a small hotel in the Latin Quarter of Paris, just around the corner from Notre Dame.

Nonetheless, a part of me always regretted not finding out just how far I could have gone in cricket or table tennis.

Little did I know that nearly two decades later, I'd be supporting my family by specializing in another up-and-coming paddle sport...

I first started playing pickleball when my wife and I moved to a remote island community made up of mostly retirees in Puget Sound, Washington.

Like many, we were tough sells at first. "*Pickle*ball? With a *wiffle* ball? Played by all these *old* people?" We were skeptical.

And then, like many, after our first day playing, we were converts. We went out and bought all our own equipment that very same night. From that point on, our life started to revolve around pickleball (we'd even plan business meetings around our playing schedule).

About a year and a half later, the man who introduced us to the game invited me down to the first national tournament in Surprise, Arizona, when he found himself in a pinch for a partner.

Again, *little did I know...*

We had absolutely no idea what to expect, but I'll never forget that year at Nationals. My wife managed to walk away with a gold medal in her age group (there were only two teams in the 19-34 women's doubles age category back then).

But, mainly, as I like to say, we got our *derrières* kicked.

"Dink? What's that?"

"What do you mean I have to put my paddle up?"

"Yikes, that was my favorite shot! How'd they return that one so easily?"

We were in WAY over our heads and *loving* it.

That week, what had been a passionate hobby turned into a fevered addiction.

We were long done with the cold, overcast northwest weather and had rented our house out for a year, leaving us footloose and fancy free. So, naturally, we left the national tournament and headed due west to the land of perfect weather and plenty of pickleball: San Diego.

In a matter of weeks we found a free living arrangement in exchange for helping a woman out around the house. Translated, that meant: pickleball, pickleball, pickleball!

We'd get up in the morning, help her out, and head to the courts by 8 a.m. We weren't always the first people to arrive, but we were always the last to leave. With two of us and one other nutty player, we could always talk a fourth into playing until 2 or 3 o'clock in the afternoon—sometimes even playing in the rain! (We called it "puddle ball.")

That winter and spring, we played about 35 hours of pickleball *per week*. We'd talk to friends and family, and we really only had one thing to discuss: pickleball.

We had seen a whole new level of play at Nationals and we were determined to return the next year and play better. Needless to say, our game improved pretty quickly with that kind of practice.

For the next couple years Wendy and I traveled around the country playing pickleball and competing in tournaments from coast to coast and north to south.

In 2011, when we got pregnant with our daughter, we settled back down in San Diego to nest.

One day, I happened to play pickleball with a man (now a good friend) who had just taken an expensive lesson from a pickleball coach and was struggling terribly to hit the ball as he'd been instructed. I offered him some pointers, which quickly helped address his challenges, and the rest, as they say, is history...

(Incidentally, he was the one, a few months later, who first referred to me as "The Pickleball Guru.")

Let me pause for a second right now and say that I'm giving you more background information than I usually include in the introduction to my clinic, but I do try to cover most of the highlights.

Once my introduction is over, most people expect me to start lecturing. But here's what makes my clinic different (and why I've been told that my teaching style is something like Socrates meets Dr. Spock).

I don't tell you what *I* think.

I ask you what *you* think.

So I'll start out by asking, "What are the first three shots of the game?"

And, eventually, someone will answer, "Serve, return of serve, and the third shot."

"Exactly!" I'll say.

Then I'll go on to ask, "Now, what makes for a good serve?"

Segment 1: A Good Serve

Think about it. What would *you* answer?

At a clinic, voices will usually call out one after another, "Fast."

"Hard."

"Lots of spin."

"Over the net." (Always good.)

"In the court." (Also extremely important.)

"Deep."

I'll listen, inviting more and more answers until nobody's got anything left to add.

And then I'll ask another question.

"So, if you are playing against an opponent who is *able* to return a hard, fast, or spin-y serve, then what's the advantage of hitting hard, fast, or spin-y?"

People are usually a little stumped at this point.

What IS the advantage of that kind of serve, if you know your opponent is capable of returning it?

Slowly it dawns on people: There *isn't* much of an advantage...

Hmmm...

Then I remind people about the #1 Rule of Smart Pickleball™.

The #1 Rule of Smart Pickleball™. Always choose the shot that buys you more time so you can get into position and be ready for the next shot.

So then I ask, "What kind of serve would buy you the most time to prepare for the next shot?"

And the answers I get are something like, "Slow."

"Deep."

"A lob serve."

At which point, I get to congratulate my brilliant students, because that is *exactly* the type of serve that we will then spend the next 20-25 minutes practicing: slow, deep, and lob-like.

When people realize that I am advocating for a high, deep, "loopy" serve, as I call it, their first concern is usually, "But I love my fast serve!"

And I say, "Well, then keep it! Remember, I'm not saying anything I teach is *THE* way, I'm just showing you *A* way. Practice the high, loopy serve today, and simply add it as another weapon to your arsenal. Mix them up when you play, and pay attention to the results."

Then I'll ask, "So, what's the advantage of a slow serve?"

Someone who's been paying close attention will answer, "It gives you more time to get ready for the next shot."

"Absolutely," I answer. "And what else?"

Now they have to do a little more thinking.

Eventually, someone guesses, or I point out, that when you hit a hard shot, the opponent really just needs to block the ball and the momentum will carry it back over the net. When you hit a slow serve, not only are you saving yourself a little energy, but it forces your opponent to have to expend some energy to give the ball enough "oomph" to go over the net.

Then I dig a little deeper and ask, "Now, a slow serve gives you more time to get ready and makes your opponent work harder, but why make it a high, loopy, lob-like serve?"

With some more back-and-forth discussion, we'll usually get to the answer: A high serve bounces higher than a low, slow serve.

Most people are ready to hit a return of serve that is somewhere around their knee to waist level. But a high, loopy serve will often bounce above the waist, almost to chest level, which sometimes forces people to "chicken wing" the shot, where their elbow is out to the side and their wrist is somewhere near their armpit. In this awkward position, they are lucky to return the ball at all let alone make an excellent return.

Then we go on. "...And why do you want to hit the serve deep?" I ask.

That brings us to Rule #2 of Smart Pickleball™.

Rule #2 of Smart Pickleball™: Always choose the shot that keeps your opponents toward the back of the court.

Now, of course, against some players who are particularly immobile, a short serve may win you point after point, but for one thing, it's kind of obnoxious to do that in recreational play.

More importantly, against better players, a short serve is just an open invitation for your opponents to go directly on the offensive, putting you immediately on the defensive. If a good player sees that you consistently hit your serve short, not only will they be ready for it, but you'll be giving them a head start on getting up to the net.

The deeper you can hit your serve, while still reliably keeping it in play, the farther back you push your opponent from the net. An opponent who is not used to your deep serves may even have to take a step backward in order to hit the ball, which again, keeps them from hitting as good of a return.

Make sense?

Around this point in the clinic, we'll start to get into the specifics of how high and deep the serve should go.

I tell them to aim for the peak of their lob to be above the opponent's kitchen line, and about 10'-12' high. This will ensure the ball lands deep enough (about 2'-3' from the opponent's back line) and that it will have a nice high bounce.

Because we usually have about six people per court, I'll bring up a couple volunteers to show how the drill rotation will work. I know that at first you might be scratching your head, thinking *Six people per court! How does THAT work?!* But I promise you, I've done many clinics this way now and it works just beautifully.

For this drill, they simply line up three on each end of the court and take turns serving. Of course, I'll ask them to switch from the even court (right-hand side of the court) to the odd court (left-hand side) about halfway through our allotted time.

Below is your at-home description of the drill we'd do if you were really attending my clinic.

Now, if you want to get a feel for the physical workout my students get during an actual clinic, from the comfort of your own chair, simply flex the left and right sides of your *derrière* about 100 times each as you read through this drill.

(Just joking! If you really want to get a feel for the physical workout my students experience, get your *derrière* off your chair, out on the pickleball court, and start PRACTICING!!)

The Guru's Drill: Serving

Materials

- Masking tape or chalk
- Hula-hoop (optional)

Basic

Place a strip of masking tape or a line of chalk parallel to and approximately 30" from the back line of one side of the court.

Then, from the other side of the court, practice hitting a high, slow serve so it lands between the tape and the back of the court. Aim for the center of the service box.

Specifications for the Serve

- The peak of the arc of the ball should be approximately 10'-12' high. (This will give you the high bounce when it lands.)
- The apex of the arc should be above the kitchen line of the opponent's side of the court.
- The ball should land about 2'-3' from the opponent's baseline.

Do this exercise until you can hit 10 serves in a row into the space between the tape and the baseline.

Optional: Have your coach, assistant, friend, grandchild, or peon stand near the tape and call out "Short!" "Deep!" or "Good!"

depending upon whether your serves are shorter than the tape, deeper than the baseline, or exactly where they should be.

Advanced

Instead of the tape, find a hula-hoop from a yard sale or dollar store. Place the hula-hoop at the back of the receiving box and aim your serves inside the hula-hoop. Vary the position of the hula-hoop to target your opponent's forehand and backhand.

••

While students are drilling during a clinic, I travel from court to court doing one of the few things I won't be teaching in this book (because I wouldn't know where to begin).

When I watch someone play, whether it's pickleball or tennis, table tennis or even cricket, my mind just *does its thing* and I can't explain how.

Somehow, I can pick up on the angles of a player's body—their head, their knee, their ankle, and their wrist. *At the same time*, I see the ball, its trajectory, and the positioning of all the players on the court. And *at the same time*, my brain is compiling a database of how that shot compares to all the previous shots they've hit, along several variables.

And most of the time, *at the same time*, I can see exactly what they need to change in order to get the result that they want, whether it's a question of strategy, positioning, or technique. (I can't tell you how many times my wife has heard me telling the U.S. Open tennis players (via my TV, mind you) to stop hitting to so-and-so's forehand or to get ready for so and so to hit cross court every fourth time he goes down the line...)

So *that's* what I do during this part of the clinic.

I offer encouragement to those who are hitting great serves, and I provide feedback to those who are struggling. Again, this is part of what I offer that is precisely the opposite of a one-size-fits-all approach, because I can give each person the exact feedback they need based on what I see happening when they hit the ball.

> *"I just finished the clinic and a private lesson! I found that it takes a SPECIAL gift to observe, then transfer what you saw to your student in a manner in which it makes sense for them.*
>
> *Prem has that gift. What I learned today was extremely helpful in me understanding the nuances of the game of pickleball. The explaining of how, when, and why was invaluable!"*
>
> —Manuel Bustos | Surprise, AZ

It's always interesting to see how slowly or quickly people are able to pick up on the serve I teach. Because it doesn't demand any fancy wrist-work or extraordinary strength, it's often the newer or more timid players who get the hang of it right away, while a number of extennis players just keep wincing as I ask them to hit the ball higher, slower, or deeper.

(I know I rag a bit on tennis players, but truly, I love them. They can quickly become the best pickleball players, but only once they finally acknowledge that pickleball is actually a different sport with different equipment, different rules, and therefore different strategy, than the sport they have been playing and loving all their life.)

Here's what one student wrote to me after a clinic like this.

"Prem, it was really worthwhile for me to be in your class last Saturday. Of course, you immediately robbed me of what I thought was the strongest part of my game—my hard, spinning serve, but I definitely understand your rationale.

Last night, I practiced your long, deep, slow serve, but I also laced it with a few of my hard serves. Interestingly, people had a harder time returning the serve you taught me. And, as you said, it gave me more time to get myself set into position."

– John Croes | Melbourne, FL

After drilling on the serve, we regroup for the next segment. Maybe you can guess what happens next.

Segment 2: A Good Return of Serve

I'll ask, "So, what do you think makes for a good return of serve?"

By this time, most people have caught on and are thinking about the Rules of Smart Pickleball™.

It doesn't take long for people to guess, "Deep!"

"Slow!"

"High!"

"Yes," I answer, "and you can do that by either getting beneath the ball and scooping it up, or by holding your paddle down to hit a half-volley as it rises off the bounce."

We don't spend nearly as much time talking about the return of serve as we did talking about the serve because they've already got the idea, and I soon send them back out to do some more drills on the return of serve.

The Guru's Drill: Return of Serve

Materials

- Masking tape, chalk, or hula-hoop

Basic

Place a strip of masking tape or line of chalk parallel to and approximately 30" from the back line of one side of the court.

Now have someone serve to you from the side of the court with the tape or hula-hoop, and practice hitting a high, slow return of serve so it lands between the tape and the back line on their side of the court.

Have your practice partner call out "Short!" "Deep!" or "Good!" depending on whether your returns are shorter than the tape, deeper than the baseline, or exactly where they should be.

Ask them to vary the type of serve and notice which are easier or more challenging for you to return.

Do this until you can hit 10 return of serves in a row that all land within the target zone.

Specifications for the Return of Serve

- The peak of the arc of the ball should be approximately 10'-12' high. (This will give you the high bounce when it lands.)
- The apex of the arc should be above the kitchen line of the *opponent's* side of the court.
- The ball should land about 2'-3' from the opponent's baseline.

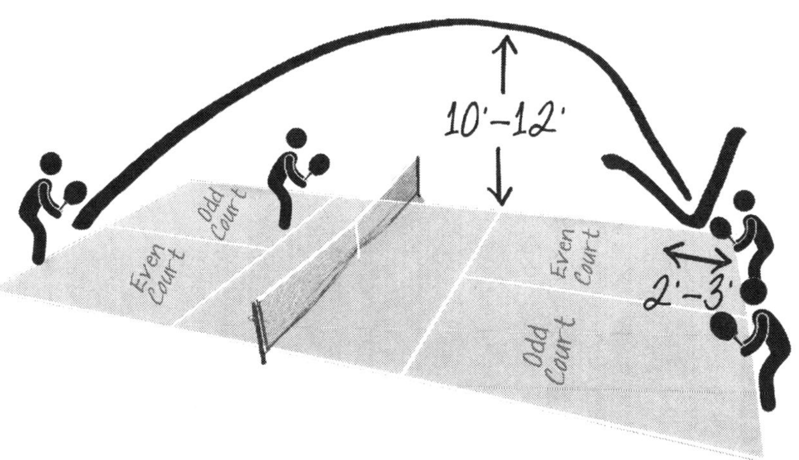

Advanced

Instead of the tape, place a hula-hoop at the back of the server's box and aim your returns inside the hula-hoop. Vary the position of the hula-hoop to target forehand and backhand.

Now, this is another point where it gets kind of fun to watch the drills. This is when the people who were most skeptical about the high, deep, slow serve find out just how much trouble they have returning it during the drills.

This is where the tables start to turn because the people who may not be the fastest or the strongest or the youngest in the group start to see how they can still have a chance at competing with and even beating the others.

This is where participants in the clinic really start to understand the power and potential of playing *Smart Pickleball*™.

> *"Prem, I just wanted to let you know that the class you gave my son and I has made a big difference in my game. I started playing in July of this year and really enjoy playing but the strategies that you taught me have changed my game. I look at playing in a new light. Using these strategies and skills has made me a better player. I look forward to entering some tournaments this coming year. My son has never played and you were able to take his tennis skills and turn them into pickleball skills. I look forward to my next trip to San Diego and another lesson. Thank you again."*
>
> – Doug Bare | Cheyenne, WY

Segment 3: A Good Drop Shot

When we come back together for our last exercise of the day, I say, "Well, we've covered the first two shots of the point with the serve and return of serve. Now, tell me, what would you say is an ideal third shot?"

People call out:

"A lob shot."

"A hard drive down the middle."

"A hard drive down the line." (I'll always ask these people if they are long-time tennis players and the answer is inevitably, yes.)

"A drop shot."

"Alright, and to quote (or perhaps misquote) the legendary Mark Friedenberg, 'The third shot is whatever you need it to be, depending on where your opponents are.' If your opponents are staying back, a hard drive might work. If you're caught off balance and a lob is all you can hit, so be it. But if you're playing against good players who are up at the net before you even hit your shot, you're dealing with what I (and the man who taught me the game) call 'the critical third shot.' So let's see how some of your responses hold up for that critical third shot."

Then I take these answers one by one, and offer some demonstrations. I call up a volunteer who is about my size and height and say, "Let's start with the lob shot."

We stand at the kitchen line and I ask the volunteer to hold up his paddle as high in the air as he can while I do the same. I show how either of us can easily take two steps backward from the kitchen line, and we can cover about 8' of vertical space with no problem, blocking off most of the court.

For the opponents to hit *over* us and still land *in*, they really have to hit a perfectly executed lob, which is not an easy task. It's not a high-percentage shot.

Of course, against players who are less mobile, you may get away with it, but in terms of playing Smart Pickleball™ against better players, it's just not a great strategy.

"So, let's look at a hard drive down the middle or down the sideline..."

I'll ask my volunteer to join me again at the kitchen line. We have our paddles up and in the ready position. Then we take turns, extending our paddles as far left and right as we can reach. Together, we can cover well over 75% of the width of the court when we are at the kitchen line. I point out that if you're playing against opponents who are ready at the net, they'll just return a hard shot back at you as fast or faster than you hit it at them.

A hard shot, whether it's down the line or the middle, violates the #1 Rule of Smart Pickleball™, remember? It doesn't buy you any extra time to get ready for the next shot.

So, no hard shots for your third shot.

Now, on to the next suggestion, the drop shot.

If my volunteer partner and I are standing up at the kitchen line with our paddles at the ready, and someone hits a drop shot that lands inside the kitchen, it forces us to let the ball bounce. During the time it takes to bounce, the opponents have just bought themselves plenty of time to get up to the net and prepare for the next shot. That's playing Smart Pickleball™.

So let's say that either from your own experience or through our discussion in the clinic, you understand and buy in to the concept that in order to win a pickleball game against better players:

- You gotta get up to the net and
- The best way to get up to the net from the back of the court is to take advantage of the no-volley rule by hitting a drop shot, and rushing to the line while your opponent is letting the ball bounce.

As I'm sure you'll be the first to admit, understanding the concept intellectually is a far cry from being able to physically implement it. Many people struggle with figuring out how to hit a drop shot that actually drops *out* of their opponent's wheelhouse and *doesn't* go into the net.

4 Secrets to Get Your Drop Shot to Go Where You Want (and Not Where You Don't)

Here are my four secrets to get your drop shot to go where you want (and not where you don't). In a clinic, I'll usually demonstrate these before sending students out to practice.

#1: Hit the Ball Just Before the Second Bounce

After the return of serve, you actually have much more time than you expect to hit the ball before it bounces again.

Many players try to take the ball after the bounce and before the ball reaches the top of the next arch. But in order to get the most control of your shot, you need to wait and hit the ball AFTER it has passed the top of the arch, while it's on its way back down, and right before it is going to make a second bounce.

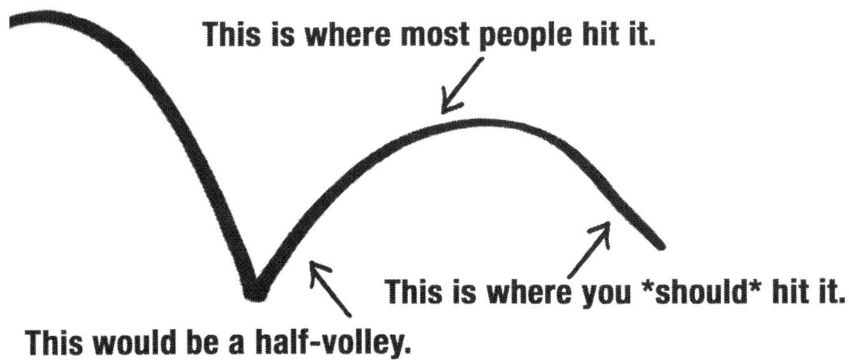

Now, I realize this is a question of seconds or milliseconds, but it really will make a big difference the longer you can wait to hit the ball.

This gives you more time to see where your opponents are positioning themselves, so that you can place the ball where they are not. Plus, the ball has also slowed down considerably by the time it gets there, so you have less speed to counteract, giving you more control.

#2: Lift with Your Knees

One time when I played and spectated at the Grand Canyon State Games in Surprise, Arizona, I made a point to pay special attention to the fact that nearly all the best players lift with their knees. No matter their height—average, short or tall, the best players all bend their knees and *lift their paddle.*

I'm not sure I can even explain the mechanics of why this is true, but when you bend your knees and use your whole body to lift your paddle and *scoop* the ball, you'll have more control than you ever thought possible.

When you bend and lift with your knees, you are forced to get your timing right. This means you're not just reaching out to get your paddle in front or unconsciously reacting to the shot, but you are positioning yourself closer to the ball and in a better position to hit it.

The improvement in your accuracy when you make the shot is absolutely worth every minute of practice to get the timing down.

#3: Don't Swing & Hit: Instead Scoop the Ball

Just put your paddle in place and scoop the ball up and where you want it to go (as you're lifting with your knees). The motion of your paddle should be more in an upward direction than a front-to-back swing.

With a deep back-swing your paddle moves along the course of several feet in just a few seconds. That range of motion of the paddle makes it very difficult to hit the ball consistently shot after shot.

When you reduce the swinging motion, you reduce the variability of your shot, and therefore make it more consistent.

If any of you have watched my friend Coach Mo's video, he talks about aiming the face of your paddle before you hit the shot, and that is the same theory—minimize the amount of motion before the ball gets to you, so that you can maximize your consistency.

So instead of swinging your paddle, imagine it was a bowling ball. Now, a bowling ball is so heavy, and has such momentum, that we really must stay in control of it while we swing the ball back, and as we push it forward. And we allow the natural follow-through of our arm after releasing the ball. That is exactly the speed, motion, and control that I want you to give your paddle while you hit your drop shot.

Try it.

#4: Aim for an Arch, Not a Dying Quail

Aim for a drop shot that has a considerable arc on it, which peaks somewhere over the kitchen line *on your side of the net* and drops across the net.

Now, this certainly isn't the ONLY way to hit a drop shot, but you'll find it gives you the greatest control and the greatest consistency.

I've already mentioned my wife, Wendy Garrido, who is an excellent 5.0 player who has taken a couple Gold Medals at Nationals for her age group and placed 4th in the Women's Doubles Open division in 2012.

Now Wendy also does most of my writing and editing so I promise you that *she* included this because she thought it would help you...

Wendy's most common way to hit a drop shot is what a friend of ours termed "the dying quail." The ball travels at a mostly horizontal trajectory until it passes the net, and then seemingly drops straight down (like a bird shot out of the air). It's a *very* difficult shot to return, but the problem is, it's also a very difficult one to hit consistently, and if she doesn't hit it exactly right, it usually lands in the net.

Instead, give yourself some wiggle room. Hit the ball so it has plenty of room over the net by aiming your arch, like I said, over the kitchen or kitchen line on your side of the court.

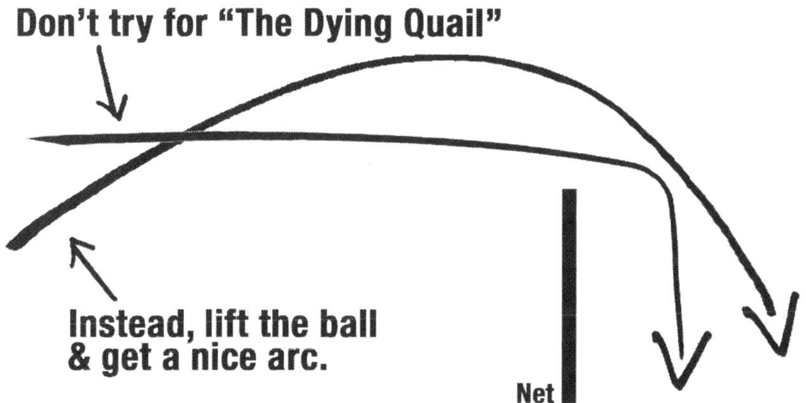

(For the record, Wendy says she does agree that my way of hitting the drop shot is more effective for her, it's simply that old habits are hard to break and she hasn't spent much time on it since we had our daughter in 2012.)

So those are my 4 secrets to getting your drop shot to go where you want (and not where you don't).

Once my students have heard these tips, I send them out for you-know-what: drills, drills, drills.

The Guru's Drill: The Drop Shot

Materials

- Hula-Hoop (or masking tape or chalk to substitute)
- Practice partner optional but recommended

Instructions

Place the hula-hoop in the kitchen zone so it is just touching the net on the opposite end of the court.

If practicing by yourself, drop the ball from chest height at the baseline, bend your knees, and after the ball bounces, lift the ball from below to scoop it over the net so it bounces in the hula-hoop.

If practicing with a partner, ask them to hit the ball deep to you at the baseline. Bend your knees and lift the ball as described above to hit it back into the hula-hoop. The advantage of having a practice partner do this is that you'll get accustomed to hitting the ball at a variety of speeds and angles.

Practice this drill on both your forehand and backhand side.

• •

Here's a comment I received from a student after working with him on the drop shot in a private lesson.

"I had heard about Prem from a friend who had highly recommended him. My friend was right!!

I signed up for a lesson when Prem visited our location. From the outset, he was interested in what we wanted to improve upon. He worked with us as a group of four and also spent individual time 'coaching' us on execution. He is a gifted instructor and has a very good communication style.

It has been two weeks since the lesson... I am thrilled with what he taught me and the results show it. I have improved my baseline drop shots dramatically and my net play has also improved. I am convinced with additional practice and confidence, it will continue to pay off.

I also highly recommend Prem for lessons and will welcome the opportunity to sign up for another when the opportunity arises. Thanks, Prem!!"

—Paul Lazdowski | Leesburg, FL

So I know you're probably not going to put down this book and go straight to the court (or maybe you will!) but did you find this section helpful? I hope it's already given you some new things to think about and I would love to hear how it goes whenever you do get off your *derrière* and out on the court. ☺

Once we wrap up the drop shot drills, we come back together to debrief and go through some general Q-and-A's.

Frequently Asked Questions: Part 1

Here are some questions that are pretty typical of what I'll hear at the end of Day 1 of a clinic.

The Drop Shot

Where Should I Aim My Drop Shot?

The most important thing is to get it shallow enough that they *have* to let the ball bounce and as *slow* as possible so you have the maximum amount of time to get to the kitchen line.

That said, I will remind you that in the center of the court, the net is a full two inches lower than on the edges of the court. Therefore, you have a much better chance of your shot going *over* the net instead of *into* the net, if you hit toward the middle of the court.

Once you have a lot of control over your shot, if you see an opponent creeping toward the middle, you may choose to place the ball toward the backhand side of their court. Remember though, that going for this shot opens you up to the chance of hitting the ball wide, which will never be an issue if you hit toward the middle.

Is There Ever a Time I Shouldn't Hit a Drop Shot?

Absolutely. When your opponent hits a short return of serve, don't go for the drop shot. Instead, hit a deep drive at your opponent's feet as they are approaching.

Remember, the drop shot is designed to be used when your opponents *are already up at the net*, but if they haven't hit a good, deep return and they aren't up there yet, then make sure to take advantage of their mistake.

The Lob Shot

I Know You Said Not to Lob on the Third Shot, But What About Other Shots?

When Is It a Good Idea to Lob?

Oh, the lob shot, is it a winning or losing strategy? Of course, whether it's boring or whether it's gratifying usually depends on whether you're the one *doing* the lobbing or the one *being* lobbed. I often get asked whether lobbing is an effective strategy, and my somewhat helpful answer is: It is unless it isn't.

Here's what I mean...

1. **It's Only a Lob Shot if It Lands In (Otherwise, It's an Unforced Error)**

A lob is obviously NOT an effective strategy if it lands *outside* of the court, causing you to lose the point. So don't lob unless it's a shot in your repertoire that you can count on. If it's not, then drill and practice until it is before you use it.

1. **... And If They Can't Smack It Back at You**

Second, the effectiveness of your lob depends VERY MUCH on the height and mobility of your opponents. A "lob" that lands in your opponent's wheelhouse is obviously not an effective lob. (I'd call it something between a "ridiculously high dink" and a "regrettably bad lob.")

Even some higher-ranked players like to hang out at the baseline and hit lob after lob, thinking that they'll eventually tire their opponents out. But if your opponents can hit an overhead off your lob, it probably wasn't very effective. A good player, once they are in the position to hit an overhead, can place the ball nearly anywhere they want: they can drop it short, hit a sharp angle, or run you and your partner off the court.

Now, since you and I aren't actually sitting out in the heat of the sun after a long morning of drilling (hopefully you're leaning back, relaxing comfortably in your easy chair), I'll go into a little more depth about the lob here than I would during an end-of-the-day Q and A session during a clinic...

When TO Hit a Lob Shot

There are the three situations where I DO recommend using the lob:

Scenario #1: Hit the Stealthy, Dink-in-Disguise Lob Shot

This is when you and your opponents have gotten into a dinking match and they are getting predictable. Wait 'til the moment when they are leaning a little too far forward, or getting a little slow moving back to the ready position. Then, using the exact same motion you would have used to hit a dink, give the ball some extra loft, and have it go well over their heads into a beautiful lob, which they can't get back for because they were too far committed to a dink.

Scenario #2: Hit a Defensive Lob Shot at the Net

The right time to go for the defensive lob is when you are rushing to the net to get a short ball going at a sharp angle off the court, and you're not likely to be able to keep your dink low. A high, deep lob forces your opponent back from the kitchen line, giving you time to get back in position and prepare for the next shot.

Scenario #3: Hit a Defensive Lob Shot to Counter a Lob

Find out more about this one below.

What to Do When Your Opponents Hit a BAD Lob Shot

If the lob is going to land too deep, don't hit it. (I know, a tough one, right?) Instead, let it bounce, call it out, and congratulate yourself on being smart enough not to hit an out ball.

If the lob is too low, and your opponents are deep, smack it with an overhead right down the middle of the court. If they are at the net, smack it at their feet or in the middle of the court.

What to Do When Your Opponents Hit a GOOD Lob Shot

First, get clear on your mobility level.

If you don't feel comfortable turning around and running to the back of the court, don't bother running for lobs. For most intermediate players who aren't very mobile, once you know that your opponent is a consistent "lobber," you can hang farther back on the court, so that it's harder for them to hit a good lob, forcing them to play in front of you. If your opponents only occasionally hit a lob, and you don't have the "wheels" to run after them, simply applaud your opponent and say, "Good lob." It's simply not worth the risk of injury.

If you feel fairly comfortable going back for a lob and your partner is not very mobile, then just decide to do your best and go after all the lobs.

If you're a more advanced player and/or playing with a partner where you both have a lot of mobility, the question is, who goes back for the lob?

Who Should Run for the Lob?

I recommend that the person who has the clear and constant line-of-sight of the ball is the person who should run for the lob. Therefore, if the lob is going over YOUR head, it's your partner who should run for the lob, while you call "switch" and slide over to take their place. If the lob goes over your partner's head, you (still) call "switch" and run back to take the lob. Because you can track the ball better, you have the best chance of being able to get back and in position to hit a decent return.

What Shot Should I Hit to Counter a Lob Shot?

So then the question arises: In the situation where you've just run back to take a lob, what is the best shot to hit?

If you CAN, the best shot to go for is a drop shot, to bring you and your partner back up to the net, but it's a *very* difficult shot at that point. This is the aforementioned Scenario #3, where the safer shot is to return with another high, deep lob, which will send your opponents scrambling to the back of the court and give you time to get back in position and move up to the net again.

I'll take one more question from the group before wrapping up for the day.

"Prem, do you have any strategies for how to keep your eye on the ball better? I find that I miss 90% of the balls that I don't watch, and yet I always seem to find myself getting distracted."

"Sure thing," I say. "I've got some, and my wife's got some good suggestions, too."

Strategies to Keep Your Eye on the Ball

"Here's what works for my wife. Have you ever watched a dog's eyes while its owner takes some bacon out of the fridge and over to the stove? They have a singular focus, smooth tracking, and never take their eye off the meat.

"If you find yourself hitting a lousy shot and then realizing that you weren't even watching the ball when you hit it, remember the dog and the meat."

There are a few chuckles from the audience.

"From the moment the server picks up the ball, imagine you're the dog and it's a piece of meat. Just track the ball from their hand...to their paddle...all the way until it bounces on your side of the court and then for the rest of the point.

"Another strategy is to look for the holes in the ball. Some people find it useful to focus on looking, not just at the ball, but at the *holes* in the ball. So that's something else that you can try."

"And lastly, I want to remind you about that obnoxious grunting scream some tennis players make. You don't have to be obnoxious about it, but if you focus on making even a quiet sound at the moment you make content with the ball, it will ensure that you are actually *looking* at the ball when you hit it. This can be under your breath, and just an "Ugh!" or "Hmm!" (or even a "*Beep!*" if you did really want to be obnoxious about it).

"My point is, it doesn't matter what you say, just focus on making a noise when you make contact with the ball and I can almost guarantee that your shots will improve."

From Clinic to Lessons

"Okay, folks, that's all we've got time for today," I say. "Get ready because tomorrow is gonna be a much harder workout than today. You're going to work those quads, so rest up tonight and I look forward to seeing you tomorrow."

By this point in a clinic, we've spent about two and a half hours together. It would be high time for you to go home, digest all this information, rest your legs, get some sleep. Of course, some of the less sensible among us actually go out and continue drilling in the afternoon.

But, really, it's not necessary. Rest and integration time are just as important to improving your game as drilling. We cover and practice a lot during the first day and there is *plenty* more to come the next day.

You, my friend, however, don't necessarily get let off quite so easily. Even if you did spend all morning out on the courts, the only muscles you're working at the moment are in your eyes and hands. So, I'm going to continue right on to a behind-the-scenes look at what happens after Day 1 of a clinic.

Once most of the students have left, I'll typically head out to lunch with one of the organizers of the clinic. This is a great opportunity to get some face-to-face time with someone who I have often talked to extensively over the phone while planning the clinic, but usually just met upon arrival the night before.

Lunch, however, is usually cut a little short by my next appointment on the courts for a private lesson. I'll sometimes have one or two private foursome lessons lined up on the day of a clinic and often up to five per day in the days following the clinic.

When I first started offering clinics and lessons, I would offer individual, pair, and foursome lessons, but it soon became clear that feeding thousands of balls per day while often hustling to return balls was simply too grueling. Even with a foursome lesson I will sometimes have all four students on one side of the net while I feed them balls, however, it is much more sustainable overall.

I've found same-skill foursome groups to be the perfect balance of being intimate enough to give lots of individual coaching and feedback, while also allowing me to work with the most people in the limited time I have available for privates.

So, hurrying from lunch, back to the courts, I'm almost always feeling excited to launch into my private lessons. Every now and again my wife asks me, "Even our two-year-old daughter knows to stand at the fence and call out to people to 'Bend your knees!' Don't you get *bored*, teaching the same clinic and telling people the same thing in privates over and over again?"

I suppose it's a hallmark of me being a coach, but I simply don't get bored. (Physically achy, worn out, and sometimes completely exhausted—yes, but never bored.)

I really do find it so rewarding to see people's eyes light up as they get new clarity on something they may have heard a dozen times but never really understood before.

Maybe for my brain, it's like every new person is a new puzzle, where I get to see what pieces need to be added or rotated to make the picture more complete.

I truly don't even feel as proud of my own medals as I do when I get an email like the one I got after my clinic and lessons in Virginia this year, listing about ten of my students who went on to win medals in a tournament that took place soon after I left.

And, when I get the emails telling me that as a result of my presence, the highest-ranked, yet most ill-mannered player at the club has now taken it upon himself to go out with a whole new attitude, to a whole new venue, and is encouragingly coaching newbies, then I know that I must be in the right place, doing something good.

So as I head back to the courts for part two of a long day, I go with an enthusiastic heart and a ready mind, if not fresh legs.

Private Lesson #1

Let's say that for the first private of the afternoon, I have a group consisting of two couples who play at about a 3.0-3.5 level. Now you can bet your booty that there are already all sorts of dynamics happening between the husbands and wives before I even step foot on the court.

So I have the sometimes delicate job of being the one to tell the wife, "No, that really *was* his ball."

Or, as nicely as possible, telling the husband, "Hmmm... It sounds like you've been telling her what to do ever since you learned to play pickleball, how's that working out for you? Not so well? Okay, well then why don't you just sit back and watch and let me talk to her about how to hit the ball... That IS what you're here for, right?"

But that doesn't usually happen 'til further into the lesson. When we start out, I gather the four players together and ask them what they want to get out of our limited time together. Sometimes they will have already agreed on a particular focus, other times I get four different people calling out four different answers.

I have a pretty good sense of how much we'll actually be able to cover in a session, and within a few minutes we come up with a customized action plan.

So let's say that in today's group, the first couple, who we'll call Maria and Rob, start out by asking, "We always seem to argue about who should hit the ball in the middle. We'd like to find out how to know for sure who should hit the ball."

"Ahhhh… Yes! And that's why they say 'Down the Middle Solves the Riddle,' I respond. "It's one that a lot of teams get stuck on. We can definitely talk about that today."

Then I arch my eyebrows inquisitively at the other couple. "She needs to work on her backhand," Gary answers.

"Ahhh...Lovely that you know what *she* needs to work on. What would *you* like to work on?" I ask.

"Oh, me? Hmm…" Gary hesitates. "Well, I really just signed up because they needed a fourth, but, um… Hmm…. You sure did make it look easy today when you were standing at the net returning those hard shots from that tennis player. I'd like to know how to do that better."

"Okaaaay, great," I say.

And then I turn the conversation back to his wife. "So, Paulette, Gary says you need to work on your backhand. I want to know, what do YOU want to get out of our time together?"

"Well, sure, I miss some shots on my backhand sometimes, but what I'd really like to work on are my volleys at the net. It seems like I have a perfect shot set up, and then I blow it."

"Okay, so it sounds like we've got a lot on the table, but I think we can make it all work. We've got Rob and Maria who want to get clearer on who hits the balls in the middle. We've got Gary here, whose generous spirit led him to say yes to being your fourth, but figures he can learn a little about returning hard shots at the net, and we've got Paulette who wants to get more consistent with her volleys. Does that sound about right?"

Everyone nods their head in agreement.

"So here's what we're going to do. First of all, I'm going to start with something that will help all of you. Now I can promise that your game will improve eighty percent *today* if you just do this one thing." Their eyes widen a little in disbelief. Gary looks particularly skeptical.

"Now I know it might sound hard to believe," I continue, "but it's true. This is what makes me look effortless when people are banging the ball at me. It's also the reason Paulette keeps missing her volleys. Rob and Maria, it's something your game needs too... Now does anyone have any idea what we're going to start working on?"

They look at me rather blankly.

"Today, we're going to work on keeping your paddle up."

Keep Your Paddle Up—No, Really!

I hear a little guffaw from Rob. Maria says, "I'm pretty sure I already do that, ever since I saw a video online that talked about it."

"Great, I say. Well, we'll do some drills and as soon as you each show me that you're holding your paddle up consistently, we'll move on. So Gary and Paulette, I want you to come over here with Maria and Rob," I say, "and I'm going to step over here to the other side of the net."

We're going to start with some dinks but first I ask them to show me their ready position.

They each bring their paddle up to varying degrees. Their paddles are all in the range between bad and ugly.

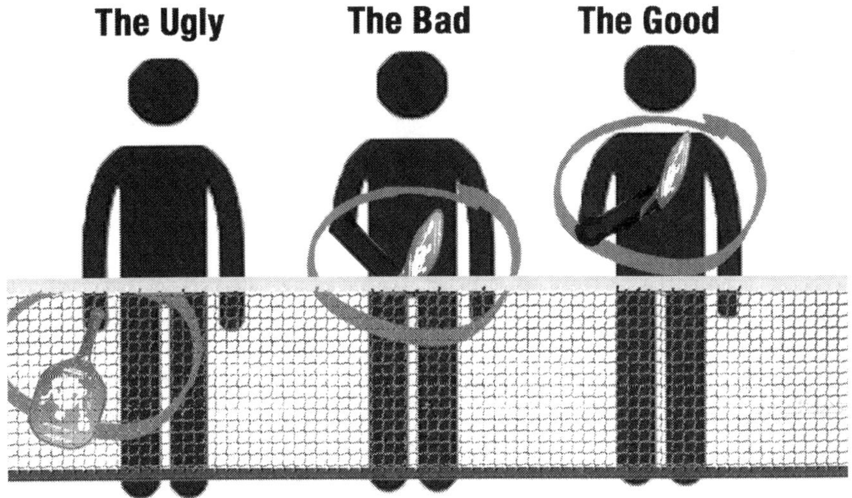

(On a side note: I considered adding a fourth diagram to the image above, which I would have called "The Friedenberg" after Mark Friedenberg, one of the legends of pickleball. Mark's ready position tends to be holding his paddle up by his *ear*, which is very effective for him.)

"Now, you're standing at the kitchen line. The net is about 32"-34" tall depending on where you're positioned. Show me on your body how high the net goes." They each indicate somewhere between their belly button and their crotch.

"Okay, the net is protecting you from there down. So you need to focus on protecting yourself from that line *up*. Now show me your ready position again.

"Look what happens if someone hits a hard ball toward your torso, and your paddle is down in front of your belly. One of two things is going to happen. Either you'll direct the ball from your paddle downward, in which case it's going to land into the net, or you're going to hit it upward, in which case you'll pop it up to give your opponent an even better opportunity at the next shot."

They nod their heads in agreement, but I can tell it hasn't quite sunk in yet.

"Next we're going to practice some dinks. Your job is to *keep your paddle up* and stay ready. *Don't* fall asleep! I'll be mixing the balls up between the four of you, and if I see that you're starting to snooze, I'm going to hit you the ball. Now, if your paddle is up, I'll just dink it to you, because that's my best shot. But if your paddle is down, my best shot is going to be to smack it pretty hard at you, and we'll see what happens from there."

The women shift nervously, wondering, *Is he really gonna hit me with the ball?*

The men look confidently bored.

And then we begin.

Dink...

Dink...

Dink...

Dink...

Smack.

"But I had my paddle up!" Gary exclaims as the ball tips his paddle and goes out of bounds.

"No, Gary, if you had had your paddle up in the ready position, I wouldn't have gone for that shot. I went for it because I saw your paddle down," I answer.

"Humph," he says, and we continue.

Dink...

Dink...

Dink...

Dink...

Dink...

Dink...

Smack.

"Gosh, you got me there, Prem," Maria says, as she looks down where the ball just bounced off the center of her chest. "I guess my paddle was down..."

Dink...
Dink...
Dink...
Dink...
Smack.

This time it's Rob. "Now, Prem, I *know* I had my paddle up that time."

I show him exactly where I saw his paddle. His hands were in front of his waist, in his long-time tennis ready position, but that leaves his paddle much too low for pickleball.

In one lesson, I had a woman argue so vehemently that she did have her paddle up, that I secretly asked her friend on the sidelines to record our practice session. The next time she debated my call, I told her about the video and invited her to go watch it.

"Yes, I'm going to go prove it to you!" she called as she hurried off the court. A minute later she came over saying, "My gosh, you were right! My paddle *wasn't* up to my chest! Wow...This is really eye-opening!"

And so the drill continues for about fifteen or twenty minutes. It only takes getting surprised by a hard ball about four times each. Then, believe me, they remember to keep their darn paddle up between every shot.

It's this drill, and the muscle memory they develop during it, that has the potential to improve their game by eighty percent overnight.

The Guru's Drill: Keep Your Paddle Up

Materials

- A Practice Partner

On Your Own, Before You Get on the Court

With a paddle in your hand and NO ball, practice the motion of hitting your forehand, backhand, dink, volley, and overhead shots and bringing your paddle back up in front of you after every shot. Imagine hitting the shot and then, aloud, say, "1, 2, 3" as you bring your paddle back up to the ready position. Make the motion for each shot 5 times in a row (and bringing your paddle up in between) before moving on to the next one.

This will help develop some muscle memory of what it feels like to bring your paddle up from the various finish positions.

With a Partner

Playing on only half the court, practice dinking back and forth and focus on bringing your paddle up and out in front of you after you hit every shot. Ask your partner to shout "Paddle up!" every time they notice that you don't bring your paddle up to chest level.

Then, using half the width of the court, play out points (without keeping score!), and repeat the practice above. At a more advanced level, ask your partner to try to "tag" you, or hit the ball hard toward your chest, when they notice your paddle is down. I do this a lot with my private students and it's one of the best ways to realize how you "pay" for not bringing your paddle up.

Paddles Up On the Run!

Once you've practiced that, work on keeping your paddle up while moving from the back of the court up to the line. Have someone serve the ball to you. Hit the return, then hold your paddle up while you hurry up to the net. Repeat this practice again and again 'til it starts to feel natural.

My foursome group of the day has finally started to pay for a mistake they'd been making all along. And, just like Wendy and I suddenly started paying heavily for our mistakes that first year at Nationals, Rob, Maria, Gary, and Paulette made a huge leap in just the first part of our lesson.

Then we go on to our next drill.

"Now, I want you all to keep this drill in mind, and *keep your paddle up* through everything else we do today, got it?"

They nod eagerly. Something has already shifted. From Gary, who "was only here to be a fourth" to Rob, who thought he knew everything from his tennis background, this whole group is now convinced that I actually have something to teach them that they don't already know, and now they are ready to learn.

"So, I want to return to Maria's question about who should take the ball when it's in the middle. There are two important parts to this answer. The first is a more objective answer to who *should* take the ball, given the dynamics of the point. The second focuses on how to strengthen partner communication so that you both have more clarity, no matter who is going to take the ball."

How to Know Who Should Take a Ball Down the Middle

Now, before we continue, I want to ask you, my reader, how many times have you had your opponents hit a great shot *down the middle*, where you and your partner just watch it go by?

And how many times have your opponents hit a great passing shot *down the line*, while you were trying to cover the middle?

You, like Maria, might be wondering, how ARE you supposed to know when to cover the middle and when to cover the line? (Because, if you haven't noticed, even as small as a pickleball court is, it's hard to cover both at the same time.)

Here's the secret:

Cover the line when the ball is being hit by the opponent directly opposite YOU.

When the ball is being hit by the opponent directly opposite YOU, cover your line and let your partner cover the middle, as shown in the diagram below.

Ball Is Opposite You: Cover Your Line

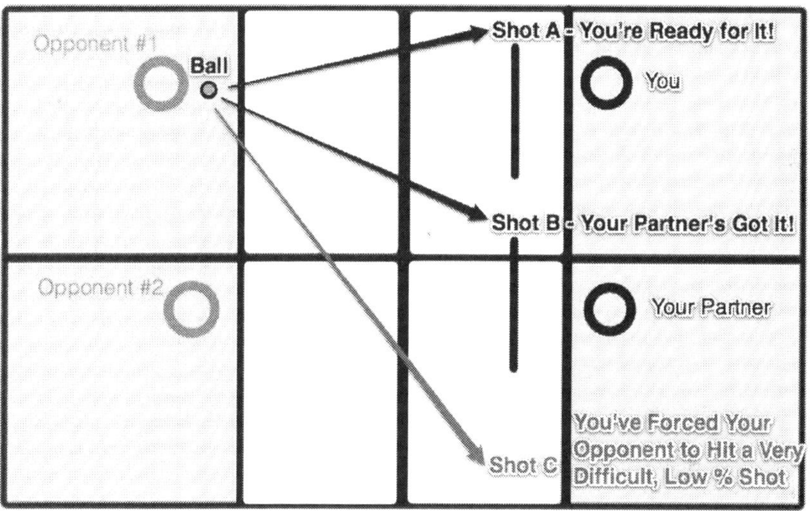

Cover the middle when the ball is being hit by the opponent directly opposite YOUR PARTNER.

When to Cover the Middle...

When the ball is being hit by the opponent directly opposite YOUR PARTNER, cover the middle while your partner covers their line, as shown in the next diagram.

Ball Is Opposite Your Partner: Cover the Middle

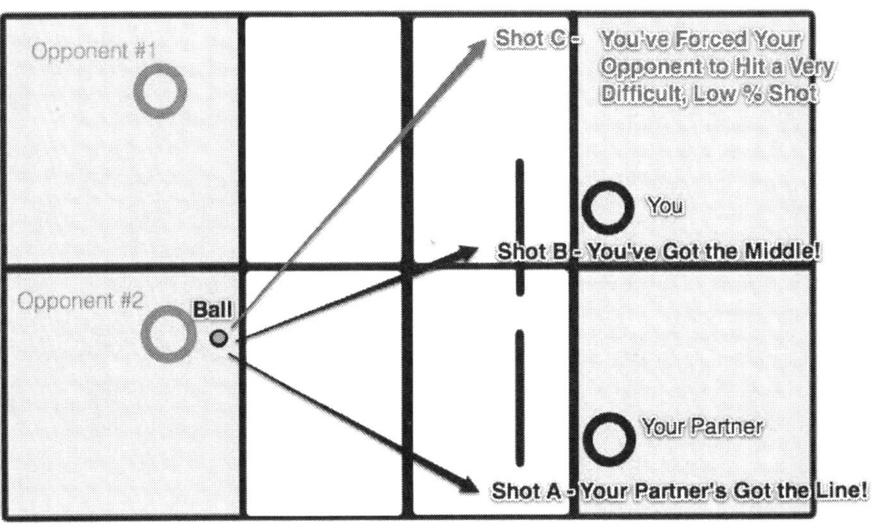

When, together with your partner, you cover the line and the middle, the only shot that your opponent has available, which isn't covered, is a very difficult cross-court shot that is a low percentage shot. (Remember, the net is about two inches higher on the sides than in the middle, so chances are good that it will go into the net or too wide.)

The wider the ball is toward the outside of the court (as in the first diagram), the more important this strategy is. When the ball is closer to the middle of the court, as in the second diagram, you and your partner can shift your positioning slightly more toward the middle of the court.

Just remember that if one of you shifts and one doesn't, you will have left a large hole in the middle of your court, which is bad news!

(Of course, this pickleball strategy works best if your partner knows when to cover the line and when to cover the middle, so don't forget to recommend this book to the person you play with most.)

"Okay, Prem, that makes sense to me," Maria says. "But what do I do if I'm covering my line on my forehand side like you said, but my opponent hits that difficult cross-court shot to my partner's backhand and makes it?"

"Well, Maria, first...Give yourself a pat on the back," I say, "because if that happens, you are most likely playing against the top fifteen percent of players in the country right now (seriously). Then, get your mind back on the game. Your partner should hustle over to catch that ball after the bounce, and you should slide back over to cover the middle again.

"This might be a good opportunity for your partner to hit the ball down the line if the person opposite them doesn't look ready for that shot, or if they DO look ready for that shot, your partner can just gently dink the ball back over the net toward the middle of the court."

I can tell there's a lot of mental processing happening when Rob asks, "But, Prem, when it's my forehand in the middle, why should Maria cover the middle with her backhand?"

"If your forehand is in the middle, that means any shot down the line is going to your backhand side. That is a tough enough shot to get if you are near the line, but there is no way you can cover the line WITH YOUR BACKHAND if you are standing near the middle of court trying to hit a ball that is within your partner's reach.

"Remember, you need to be toward the middle when the ball is opposite your *partner*, but when the ball is opposite YOU, if you're near the middle, you've just given your opponent at least five feet of net that is WIDE OPEN.

"Make sense?"

They get it intellectually. Now it's time to help them integrate it into their game, so I ask them to play out a few points without keeping score.

● ●

The Guru's Drill: Shadowing Your Partner

Materials

- Your partner and at least 1 other player
- Masking tape
- A timer
- Optional: string approximately 12'-15'

Instructions

Using a small piece of masking tape, mark the center of the left and right halves of the court at the no-volley line (as shown by the white dots in the diagram below).

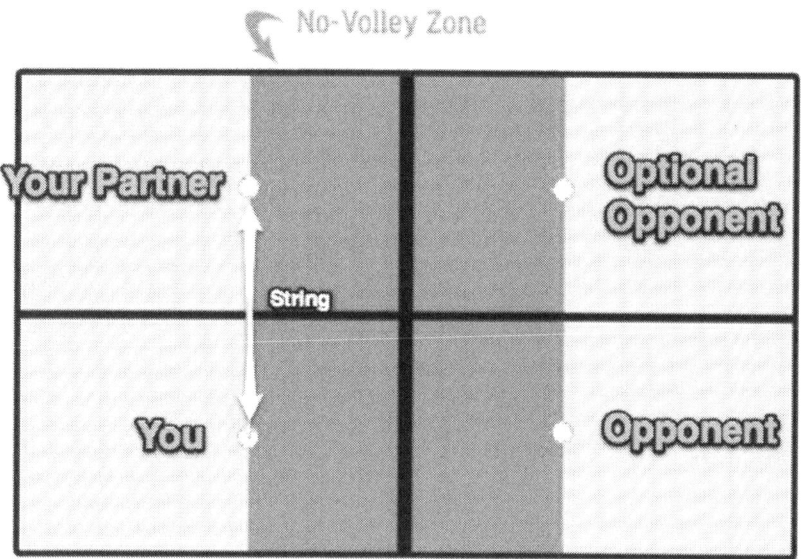

Optional: *Have you and your partner each stand on the tape you've marked on each side of the court. Tie the string around your waist to your partner's, so that if your partner moves to the left side of the court, you are forced to move an equal distance to the left.*

Part A

Have your partner practice hitting dinks back and forth cross-court across the net to your opponent (opponent should be opposite *you* if there are just 3 of you).

Each time your partner moves to get a ball, you should move with them. EQUALLY AS IMPORTANT, when they come back in to position to the center of their side of the court, you should move back to the center of your side of the court.

The ideal foot movements are a series of small, shuffling, side-to-side steps. If you hear your shoes moving across the court every time your partner hits the ball, you're doing it correctly.

Then, switch so that you are hitting the cross-court dinks, and have your partner move to the left and right as you hit the ball.

Part B

Now, set your timer for about 1 minute.

Have your opponent serve the ball to play out a point. Play the rally as usual until the timer goes off, when you should all freeze. Look down and see where you are each positioned relative to the tape marks you placed on the center of each half of the court.

It's amazing how quickly we can forget what we practiced in just a minute of real playing!

Set the timer again for a slightly longer or shorter interval (as feels appropriate) and repeat 5-7 times, freezing to check your position each time the timer sounds.

Lastly

Believe me, I know it's a heckuva lot more work to move back to position every single time your partner returns a dink, and then to go back to shadow again each time the ball goes back to him, but if you don't, and you stay planted at the "T" in the center of the kitchen line, a good opponent will hit a shot straight down your line, which you won't be able to reach.

If you can't sustain moving completely back into position each time, at least take one good size step sideways and mentally cover your line so you are prepared for when your opponent goes for it.

••

Depending on where the ball bounces during the drill, I'll call out, "Paulette! Slide over and cover your line, missy!"

Or, "Gary, where's your paddle? If it had been up, you would have had that one, get it up!"

Or, "Rob, stay awake! If the ball is in front of Maria, that's when you need to cover the middle."

Soon they start to see how it makes sense and afterwards I ask what they learned.

Paulette says, "Gosh, between keeping my paddle up and knowing when to shift left or shift right, I was able to return those shots from Rob that I normally would have mis-hit and would have gone out."

"Yeah," Rob says, "I am used to being able to score some shots down the line, but today Paulette and Gary were like a solid wall. It seemed like they were ready for my every shot."

"Thank you so much for coming to Poway and teaching us the 'serve and return' class. 'Lofty' shots are foreign to me, so as great as I might think I am a server (I really thought I was!), this certainly was an eye opener.

I am grateful we had a fun group and enjoyed your relaxed, calm and non-critical style of teaching. We all basked in your 'Perfect!' response when we finally got it right, however the 'Short!' made us cringe and laugh at each other. I think I got it after the 40th time. I need to learn patience it seems. We look forward to our next class...

Again, thank you so much for coming."

— Cathy Visconte | Claremont, CA

"Great," I say. "Now there's just one last thing I want to remind you all about, which will really help you play better with any partner, whether it's your hubby, your wife, or somebody else.

"As we've already talked about today, a soft or hard shot down the middle often leaves your opponents both thinking the other person was going to get the ball and as a result of a lack of communication, neither of them gets it. Score one for your team!

"Of course, it's fantastic when it's your opponents who are confused. On the other hand, it's frustrating and sometimes embarrassing when you and your partner are the ones to be confused.

"Equally as frustrating is the situation in which you are all set up to make an excellent shot and your partner goes in to make a less-than-stellar smash into the net. (Not to mention—AHEM!!—the case in which you are the one to take a great shot from your partner...)"

Rob and Gary both look somewhat guiltily down.

"So what's the answer to these pickleball conundrums? One of the best solutions is partner communication."

How to Call the Ball Like a Champ

"But, Prem," says Gary, "that's easier said than done, right? It's hard enough for me to concentrate on hitting a good shot, and now you want me to *talk* during my shot?"

"Yes," Paulette agrees, "I've noticed men sometimes have an especially tough time getting their brain to do two things at once..."

"Here's the good news," I say.

"First of all, you shouldn't have to talk WHILE you're hitting the ball. And second, Gary, have you managed to master being able to talk while walking?" He grins. "If not, maybe you should go work on that first," I joke. "But this isn't very different. It's just a matter of practice.

"Forgive me for stating the obvious, but if you're calling the ball WHILE you are hitting it, it is already way too late. When you call the ball, it should be just a millisecond after your OPPONENT hits the ball, and BEFORE either you or your partner is going to hit it."

So then I have them work on the following drill.

The Guru's Drill: Call the Ball

Here's what to do the next time you're out on the court:

1. Let your partner know that you are focusing on practicing calling the ball. (It's true, and anyway, it'll give you a good excuse for any balls you miss.)
2. Choose your words and tell your partner what you're going to say. I like to use "Yours!" and "Mine!" or, "Me!" and "You!" Make sure the words you use are clearly distinguishable. Don't use "I go!" because it's easy for your partner to miss the "I" and just hear "Go!"
3. After the serve or return of serve, call EVERY SINGLE BALL your opponents hit, no matter how obvious it may seem. Remember, the focus at this point isn't about communicating, it's about conditioning your brain to get used to calling the ball during a point.
4. Practice doing this during the first 3 games of the day for the next 3 days you play pickleball and I promise you'll feel more comfortable calling the ball during the point.

Of course, it's nice if you can call the ball most of the time, but eighty percent of the shots will be obvious. The great thing about practicing like this is that your brain will be in good shape to call the ball on those shots that really count—like when your opponents hit it straight down the middle."

"That really helps, Prem," Maria says after we've played out some points where they all worked on calling the ball. "Are there any other cases where we could communicate better during the point?"

"Sure," I answer. "Besides just calling 'You' or 'Me' to decide who hits the ball, you can communicate with your partner by saying, 'Lob' when you're about to hit a lob, so they know when to stay back or rush to the net. Another important one is, 'Bounce it!' when you're not sure if a ball they are about to hit is going to be out. Lastly, of course, call 'Out!' if you know that a ball they are about to hit is going out.

On a side note, one of the top players in the country and my good friend, Billy Jacobsen, can't hear a word his partner says during the game because he's deaf. Nonetheless, he always knows when his partner is ready to hit the ball because he is so attuned to his partner's posture, position, and movements.

You, too, can pay attention to the non-verbal messages you send to your partner, by leaning in, hanging back, or feigning a shot, so that your body doesn't contradict your words.

Once you've started putting these concepts to work in your pickleball game, you'll be talking like a top player—even if you don't play like one yet!

Now, I know I said earlier that you didn't get a break at the end of Day One because you aren't really participating in one of my live clinics. That said, remember that just like there's no one-size-fits-all in teaching, there's no one-size-fits-all in reading this book.

If your brain is hurting a little, take a break. Go try a couple of the drills we've already outlined before coming back to read the rest. Or maybe just get up, move your body a little, and get a snack. (Hey, don't forget I'm French...Maybe you even want to go have a little fun with your *amour*...)

Do whatever you need to do to take care of yourself and be in tip-top shape to take in the rest of the information I'm about to share in this book...

Day 2: How to Force Your Opponent to Give You a Point or Make a Great Shot

Introduction

Now, regardless of what you've done or not done between the end of the last section and this section, I want you to imagine that it's the morning after the first day of the clinic.

Your legs are slightly stiff and achy because you either wore yourself out yesterday during the morning or you went out to play again later in the day and wore yourself out that way. (You wouldn't be a true pickleball lover if it were otherwise.)

I'll welcome the group back and start by asking people what they remember from yesterday.

"You're French!"

"You met your wife in Paris!"

"You have a two-year-old daughter..."

"Yes, yes, and yes!" I'll respond. "I'm so glad you can all remember that. Now, did you happen to retain any of the information about *pickleball*?"

Some chuckles, followed by...

"Serve deep."

"Return deep."

"Make the third shot a drop shot."

"Exactamento!" I exclaim. "Now, while we're on the topic of the drop shot, I want to touch briefly on a question one of my Canadian students asked me (yet another student who is now a good buddy).

"A while back, he asked, 'Well, Prem, it's all fine and good if I make a great drop shot, but it's a tough shot to make. Obviously if it's into the net, I'm out of luck. But what do I do if it's just too high or too deep?'"

What to Do When Your Drop Shot Doesn't Drop

"Yesterday we didn't spend much time talking about what the heck you're supposed to do when it all goes wrong. 'Cause (at the risk of sounding like a fortune cookie) I predict that in the very near future you or your partner WILL give your opponents a cream-puff of a shot that is gonna result in the ball being slammed down your throat if you're not in a good defensive position. (And sometimes even if you are.)

"My first bit of advice is this: Don't run to the net like a headless chicken."

If You're Up, STAY Up & Get Your Paddle Up

"If your partner hits a lousy drop shot when you are in perfect position at the kitchen (a.k.a. no-volley) line (and you're not deluding yourself with one of the two lies I'll discuss in the next section) then make sure your paddle is up, and just STAY IN POSITION.

"You're already in a good position to see the ball and the court and you won't have time to back-track anyway, so stay there, get your paddle up, and keep your eye on the ball."

If You're Anywhere Other Than Up, Get BACK & Get Your Paddle Up

"If you've found yourself creeping back from the no-volley line and you know you or your partner has hit a lousy shot, then move your *derrière* BACKWARD quickly. Get about a foot or two behind the baseline and get your paddle out in front of you... preferably before your opponent has even hit the ball.

"If you are the one who hit the not-so-great drop shot, take a step or two forward and get in your ready position to try for another drop shot from this new position. If you hit that, keep your paddle up and take another two steps forward. By the third shot, you should be able to make it up to the line. The secret is to get your paddle up and get in the ready position between each shot."

The Guru's Drill: Drop It From Anywhere

Have your practice buddy volley shots at the net while you're at the baseline. Practice hitting a drop shot, moving in a few feet, hitting another, and repeating, so that you get comfortable hitting them from any distance. That way, if you don't hit a perfect one the first time, you can hit one the second or third time.

Remember, once you hit the ball and are moving forward, stop and jump lightly with you feet shoulder-width apart at the moment your opponent is contacting the ball so that you will be ready for a shot to either side of your body.

"Prem," a youngish guy calls out from the back left, "I've always subscribed to the philosophy that no matter how high my 'drop shot' or how low my lob, the best thing to do is just charge to the net with my paddle at the ready. What do you think about that strategy?"

"Hey, you know me, if you have lightning-fast instincts at the net, I say *more power to ya.* But for the rest of us, whose reflexes may not be what they used to be, or for those who simply want to play Smart Pickleball™, backing up to the baseline or taking your time to get to the net makes sense because *it gives you more TIME.* (Remember the #1 Rule of Smart Pickleball™?)"

The #1 Rule of Smart Pickleball™: Always choose the shot that buys you more time so you can get into position and be ready for the next shot.

"*Time* is the secret ingredient that will let you pick up a ball many others will miss. It is what will let you place the ball *exactly* where your opponents are not, and it is what will help you recover from a rotten shot. So when you hit a bad drop shot, do what you need to do to buy yourself some time.

"Make sense?" I ask. (That's one of my signature questions, in case you haven't noticed.)

I get many nods of agreement.

"Great," I say. "Now, remind me what the purpose of the drop shot is again?"

"To buy you enough time to move up to the net," someone will call out.

"Exactly. Now, why do you want to move up to the net?" I ask.

"So you can dink," a woman in the back offers.

"Well, yes, dinking is something you do when you're at the net, but why do you want to dink, for that matter?" I respond.

We'll have a couple more people call out good guesses.

"You guys are all on the right track. There are three main reasons why it's important to get up to the kitchen line..."

"Prem, can I just ask a quick question before you go on?" a silver-haired lady from up front calls out.

"Of course," I say, and ask her name.

"My name is Darlene. When you say to 'get up to the kitchen line,' could you be more specific about how close we should be?"

"Sure, Darlene. Well, I know that a lot of people get away with playing at half court their whole pickleball career, but if you want to improve your game (and not just keep beating the same people you always beat) you HAVE to get all the way up to the kitchen and play from *right behind* the no-volley line.

"Not ON the line, of course, but RIGHT BEHIND it. I want you to plant your feet one or two *inches* from the line and *don't move back*. Move side to side as needed. Step one foot into the kitchen to take a ball on the bounce, but whatever you do, play from RIGHT BEHIND the line."

You. Must. Get. To. The. (No-Volley) Line.

"Here's why..."

Why You MUST Play at the No-Volley Line (And 2 Lies You Tell Yourself When You're There)

Reason #1: You Can Hit the Ball DOWN

"The first reason is because when you're at the net, you can hit the ball *down*. A pickleball will never bounce as high as a tennis ball, and will rarely bounce as high as the net, so anytime you take it off the bounce, you'll have to add some loft to your return shot and effectively hit the ball on an upward trajectory."

Hitting the ball downward is always a better shot than hitting it across the net at an upward angle.

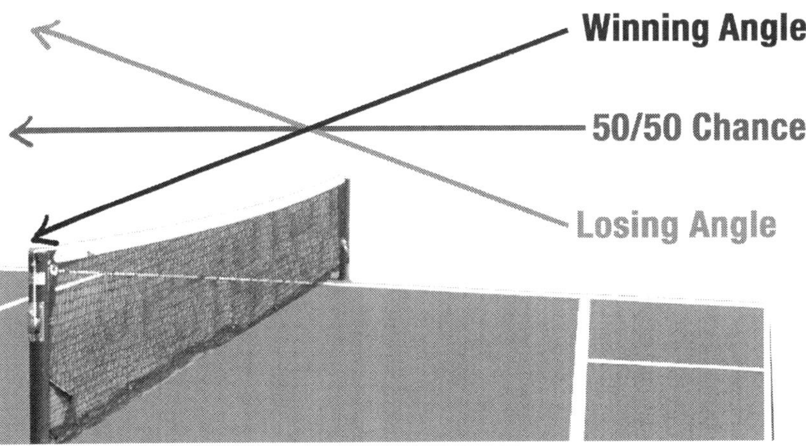

"You're much better off being as close to the net as possible so you can take the ball in the air rather than after the bounce, because a ball going at an upward angle after it crosses the net is always bad news in pickleball. I'll get into this more in the next section, but for now, remember that the farther back you move from the line, the more likely you are to have to hit the ball up. Make sense?"

I get eager nods of approval.

Reason #2: You Drastically Reduce Your Opponents' Options (And Have Less Court to Cover)

"Here's another tidbit to chew on: Because a pickleball court is only 20' wide, a doubles team at the net can effectively cover

50% of the court without moving an inch side to side (assuming even just a 5' wing span for each player). As you may know, in tennis, you can barely cover 25% of the net, so it makes sense to stay back and move laterally to cover the court, plus you have the advantage of a higher, longer bounce to give you extra time to get where you need to be.

"In pickleball, though, you don't NEED to move back to cover the court and, in fact, the farther back you are, the more angles you open up, unnecessarily giving your opponent many more options to play against you."

Reduce Your Opponent's Options By Playing at the Line

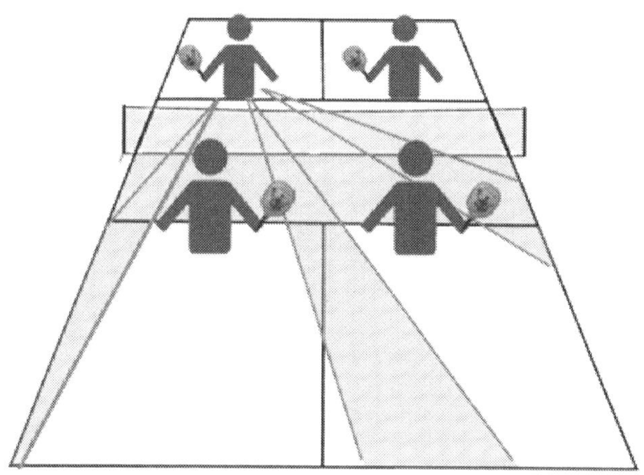

When You Play at Mid Court You Give Your Opponent More Options

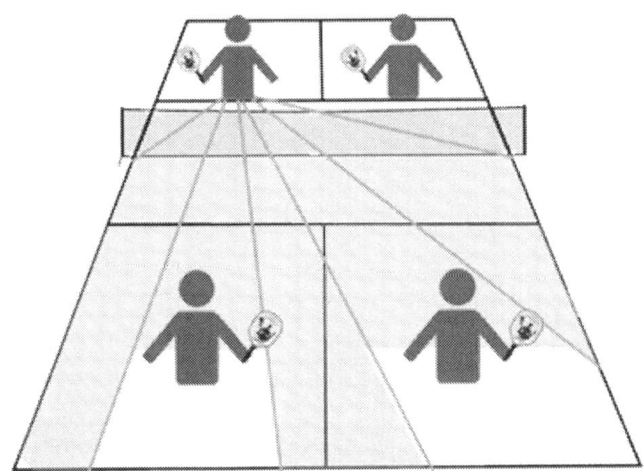

Reason #3: It Puts You On the Offensive

"And the third reason you have to get up to the net is because you can play offensively from the kitchen line. Why run around scrambling for balls your opponent hits past you when you can stay at the net and practically force them to hit a great shot or hit the ball right to you?"

"I'm not saying you can't run around like a headless chicken, make amazing defensive shots and, potentially, eventually win the point. I'm just saying it's not particularly Smart Pickleball™ and you'll never take control of the point when you're hitting from mid-court or behind."

"Playing defense like this violates Rule #3 of Smart Pickleball™: Always choose the shot or strategy that requires the least energy or effort to play out the point."

Rule #3 of Smart Pickleball™: Always choose the shot or strategy that requires the least energy or effort to play out the point.

"It's a rare shot in tennis when a player can smash the ball down on the other side or at their opponent's feet, whereas these shots are the bread and butter of a winning pickleball game (besides keeping the ball in play).

The farther you move back from the net, the less of a view you have of the other side of the court.

"That means the less likely it is you can hit a smash at your opponent's feet when they pop the ball up. Instead, you'll have to wait to hit a less offensive shot off the bounce. If you're like a lot of players, you'll try for what amounts to a line drive and swear under your breath as the ball hits the top (or even the middle) of the net."

"That all makes sense," Darlene's husband says. "Can I add one more point, though?"

"*Bien sûr...*" I answer invitingly. (That means "Of course" in French.)

"I know it may not always be the smartest move for them to make, but if you're not up to the line, isn't it easier for an opponent to drop a ball very short on you?"

"Yes...Jim, is it?" I ask questioningly. He nods. "If you're not very mobile, then you probably just lost the point. If you ARE quick on your feet, then you'll probably race in to get the ball. But chances are, as your momentum carries you forward, you will lose control of your shot and pop it up into your opponent's wheelhouse, where you'll give them a great put-away shot. If they have even a modicum of a clue about how to play the game, they will smash the ball at your feet.

"End of point. All because you chose to hang back instead of play up at the line...

"Now I will also add that many a singles player has gone far (and even won national medals) on speed alone. But doubles is a different game. If you're not at the kitchen line, you'll lose against better players.

"Every time.

"Got it? Good."

Segment 1: A Good Dink

"Now, let's take all that we've discussed so far and apply it to the dink. Just because you know to play up at the kitchen line doesn't mean you *have* to hit a dink. You *could* smash the heck out of the ball.

"In fact, I'm sure there's probably a good chunk of you who are *positive* that the dink is a shot only for sissies, weaklings, or children—and *certainly* not a shot that any man's man or woman's woman would ever hit...Am I right?"

I get more than a couple sheepish nods.

"Okay, well I hope that by the end of today you'll see the light, but if not, make sure to sign up for a private lesson with me and I'll quickly prove to you how essential—and *powerful*—the dink shot can be."

"Now, I bet there are also some of you who already understand the significance of the dink shot and have tried, to whatever extent, to incorporate it into your game, but are always on the lookout for some pointers to hit your shots more easily and more reliably, right?"

More nods.

"Our discussion and drills today should help you with that... You see, the dink shot is the answer to the drop shot. If your opponents have hit an excellent drop shot and managed to get themselves up to the kitchen line, you don't want to hit a high ball that they can slam back at your feet. Instead, you just 'dink' the ball back over the net and turn the tables on them.

"The dink shot is a slower, softer shot hit from near the no-volley line, that drops downward once it crosses the net and lands in the opponent's no-volley zone. When you hit a dink, it forces your opponent to let the ball bounce before hitting it, which usually puts them in the position of having to hit upward on the ball."

"There are two important reasons to learn to dink.

"Number one: It is a powerful strategy that better players will use against you. As a defensive strategy, if you can't at least return a dink shot with another dink without hitting the ball into the net or giving your opponent a cream-puff, you'll quickly lose the game.

"Number two: It is an excellent offensive strategy, which you can use against weaker opponents to goad them into hitting the ball into the net or giving *you* a cream-puff. Against players of equal or higher level, the dink shot gives you the opportunity to take control of the point, by defining the speed, angle, and location of the ball.

"One reason the dink gets a bad rap by all those 'macho' men is that it isn't (usually) a finishing shot. It's a set-up shot. It's the shot you play as you wait for your opponent to give you an opening where you can hit a put-away shot. To play a dink requires anticipation. It requires patience.

"Many people mistakenly believe that I am an advocate of *always* playing a soft or slow game, but really, I am advocating to be *smart* about when you go for the hard shot instead of just smashing the heck out of every single ball.

"Remember Rules #4 and #5 of Smart Pickleball™? They're about playing the higher-percentage shot and anticipating the *next shot.*"

Rule #4 of Smart Pickleball™: Always play the higher-percentage shot.

Rule #5 of Smart Pickleball™: Always anticipate your next shot as you play your current shot.

"When you're at the net, smashing a low ball is not a very high-percentage shot. Furthermore, it doesn't do anything to put you in a better position for the *next* shot. It's just not smart."

"On the other hand, the dink *puts you in control* in three important ways. First, it lets you control the speed of the ball."

Control the Speed of the Ball

"Many players are so used to defending against a hard, fast ball that the slowness of a dink will mess up their timing, causing them to make an unforced error. Learning to slow the ball down and turn your opponent's fast, hard shot into a dink does require some practice and finesse, but it IS possible and it's a game-changer once you can do it. (It's something that many of my students get MUCH better at after a private practice session.)

"Second, like we said before, the dink also lets you control the angle of the ball."

Control the Angle of the Ball

"Let's say your opponent dinks to you, forcing you to let the ball bounce. If you hit a hard shot back, it will either go into the net or go over the net at an upward angle, which is really just another way of saying a *losing* angle. Because the higher you hit the ball up, the harder and faster a good opponent will hit the ball at your feet, putting you on the defensive.

"Lastly, the dink lets you control the placement of the ball."

Control the Placement of the Ball

"When you hit a dink shot, you have more time and opportunity to place the ball where you want it. With a series of good dinks, you can move your opponents back and forth on the court until you have created an opening where you can place the ball in *just the right spot* so they can't get it.

"Okay, here's another question for you," I tell the group. "What's the difference between the drop shot and the dink shot?"

One person calls out, "They're the same thing!"

Another says, "Wouldn't it be that the dink shot is hit from the no-volley zone, whereas the drop shot is hit from the back half of the court?"

"Bingo! While the dink and the drop shot are similar in that they both head downward after crossing the net to land in the no-volley zone, the actual mechanics of hitting them are somewhat different. The drop shot is usually a more challenging/advanced shot to hit than the dink shot. So what makes for a good dink shot?"

"Low!" a dark-haired woman calls out.

"At their feet!" another says.

"Lands in the kitchen," a third says.

"Congratulations," I applaud them. "You've got it!"

Characteristics of a Good Dink Shot:

It Passes Low Over the Net

"If the dink passes too high over the net, then the ball will bounce higher than the net, allowing your opponent to hit downward on the ball (something you never want to give them a chance to do). A good dink won't bounce higher than the net, making it impossible for your opponent to hit the ball downward without hitting it into the net."

It Lands Shallow in the Kitchen

"A good dink will land in the shallow half of the kitchen. If your dink lands deeper into the kitchen or at/past the no-volley line, then it's more likely your opponent will be able to reach out and hit the ball before it bounces, which means they'll have a better chance to hit downward on the ball, and we don't want *that*, do we?"

Examples of Excellent & Good Dink Shots

Here are some examples of shots that are low over the net and/or land in the shallow half of the kitchen.

The ball can pass a little higher over the net if it is going to land very shallow, because your opponents won't be able to reach out and hit it from the air.

Examples of Bad Dink Shots

These shots are too high, too deep, or both.

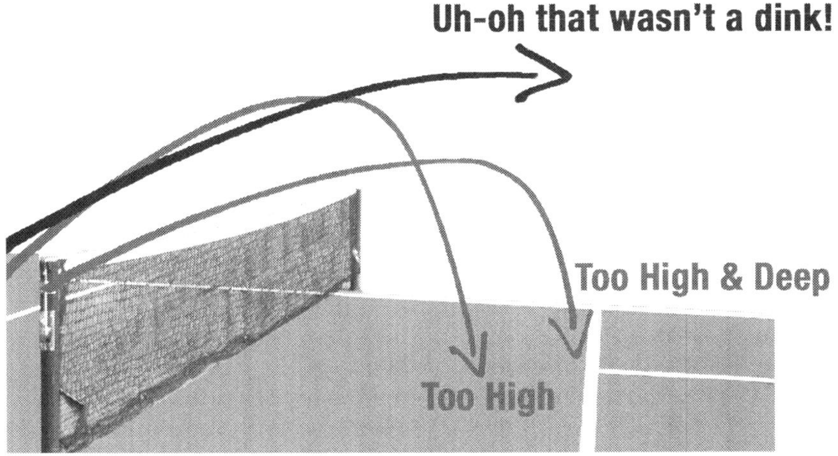

How to Hit a Good Dink Shot

Like we talked about the other day, paddle up!

Get Your Paddle Up & Out In Front of Your Chest Before & After Every Shot

"This is true for every shot, of course, but especially when you are at the net, you need to be ready for a high fast shot, *or* a low soft shot, so keeping your paddle up in the ready position between each shot is crucial.

"The other tips to hit a good dink are very similar to my tips for hitting a drop shot."

Hit the Ball Just Before the Second Bounce

"Like we talked about for the drop shot, after the ball bounces, you actually have much more time than you expect before it bounces again. Many players try to take the ball after the bounce and before the ball reaches the top of the next arch. But in order to get the most control of your shot, you need to wait and hit the ball AFTER it has passed the top of the arc, while it's on its way back down, and right before it is going to make a second bounce. Now, I realize this is a question of seconds or milliseconds, but it really will make a big difference the longer you can wait to hit the ball.

"This gives you more time to see where your opponents are positioning themselves, so that you can position the ball where they are not. The ball has also slowed down considerably by the time it gets there, so you have less speed to counteract."

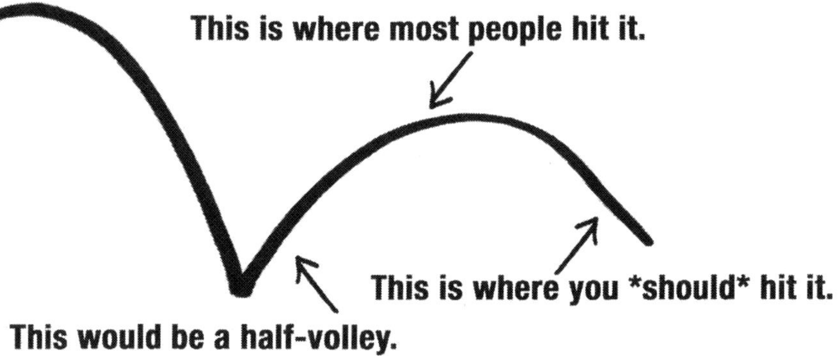

Lift With Your Knees

Don't just use your arm. Bend your knees, push down into your feet, and LIFT the ball using your whole body.

Don't Swing & Hit: Play Out In Front of You

One mistake many players make is to do a large back swing before hitting the ball. Likewise, you don't need a huge follow-through and in fact, doing so will keep you from being prepared for the next shot. Just "scoop the ball" over the net. Really, if you're hitting a dink shot, your paddle never needs to be more than about 45° left or right of front and center.

The Guru's Drill: Improving the Dink Shot

Materials

- Hula-hoops, chalk, or masking tape
- Practice partner (Recommended but not required)

Instructions

To Improve Your Placement

Place the hula-hoop (or tape) on the ground, toward the center of the kitchen/no-volley zone, positioned right up against the net. From the opposite side, practice hitting your dinks so that the ball drops into the hula-hoop. If you are practicing alone, you can drop the ball in front of you and hit it off the bounce. If you're practicing with a partner, have them watch their step around the hula-hoop and simply return the ball to you. (Or put a hula-hoop on each side so you can both practice at once.)

Shoot to get 10 dinks in a row. Then move your body 2 feet to the right and keep practicing aiming for the hula-hoop. Once you can hit 10 in a row there, move back to 2 feet to the left of your original position (so a right-handed person will be hitting a backhand), and repeat the drill.

After mastering these 3 positions, you can move the hula-hoop about 3-4 feet left and right, and repeat all 3 positions.

Eventually, you can practice cross-court dinking by having the hula-hoop against the net all the way on one side of the court, while you dink from the opposite side of the court.

To Improve Control Over the Height

Using simple quick-grip clamps (or possibly zip-ties) position the hula-hoop in a vertical position parallel to and against the net, so that approximately 1/3 to half of the hula-hoop is suspended above the net. Then practice hitting your dink above the net and through the hula-hoop.

Once you have mastered both of these drills you can combine them by aiming the ball through the hoop on the net so it lands in the hoop on the ground.

• •

As I make my rounds from court to court, one man says, "I'm surprised that it is this hard. I thought it would be pretty easy, but I just keep hitting the ball higher than I want to."

I ask him to show me a few shots.

He's doing what many players do, which is back swinging a bit, and hitting the ball from the side, rather than from below. With the angle of the wrist when you're hitting from the side, it's difficult for the stroke to continue through anywhere other than up.

Instead, I show him how to scoop the ball from underneath and in just a few shots he has considerably more control than before.

Scoop the Ball from Underneath Instead of Hitting From the Side

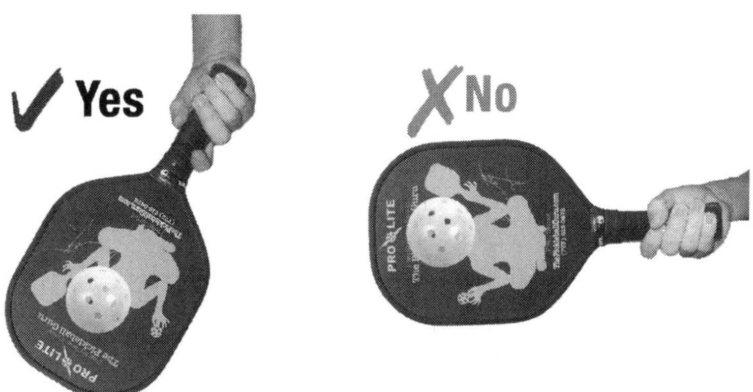

After this drill set, we come back together as usual to debrief.

"So...How'd it go?" I ask.

"My quads are hurting!" someone says.

"I never knew it was such a workout!" says someone else.

"Ah, yes… Welcome to the wimpy shot that's not really for wimps after all, eh?" I tease.

Now, the next segment will be a welcome relief for all you people who are getting antsy to (finally) give the ball a smack...

Segment 2: A Good Volley or Put-Away

I start out with a less-than-obvious question: "What's the difference between a volley and a put-away?"

"They're the same," one person calls out.

"You hit the ball downwards," another says.

"Let me ask you this," I prod. "Can you really put away a volley?"

They look at me slightly perplexed, but curious. *Where exactly is he heading with this?*

"For our purposes, the difference between a volley and a put-away is the trajectory of the ball. When you're hitting the ball horizontally, I'd consider that a volley. When you can hit the ball more downward, I'd consider that a put-away. Make sense?"

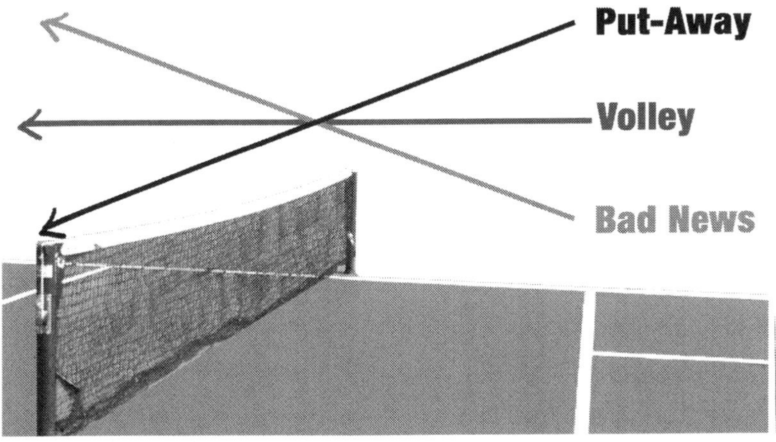

"What happens if you hit a put-away hard? Hopefully it will go at your opponent's feet and win you the point.

"What happens if you hit a volley hard? Well, if you're playing against me, I'm just gonna do my best to limbo out of the way and let your ball go flying out of bounds.

"Volleys are an inevitable part of the game, but when you hit one, you've only got about a fifty-fifty chance of winning the point.

"So the more pace you can take off your volley, the more likely it is to head downward across the net, hopefully forcing your opponent to hit upwards *just that little bit* more, until finally you get your put-away shot.

"Again, this is a game of patience. DON'T smack your volleys, DO smack your put-aways.

"Now, I want you to go back out on the court and start to dink like you were in the last drill. But instead of hitting every ball a dink, I want you to hit ANY ball you can, as a volley or put-away. Last time, you got away easy if you had a bad dink because your practice partner would just dink the ball back no matter what. This time, you're going to pay for your mistakes. (Muah ha ha ha ha!) So do your best to get your dinks as low and shallow as possible, and meanwhile, do your best to make your partner pay for their bad dinks. Got it?"

I get many nods.

"Great. Now go smack the ball, and enjoy it, 'cause you won't hear me tell you to do that too often."

The Guru's Drill: Volley Away

Materials

- A Practice Partner

Instructions

Stand 1”-2” behind the kitchen (no-volley) line at the centerline of the court and have your partner dink the ball to your left and right (near the center of each half of the court).

If Their Dink Is...

A Good Low Dink

Passing within 4-6” of the top of the net, this is an excellent shot, so just try to match it with a good dink back.

A High Dink

If it’s high enough for you to hit out of the air in front of you, their dink was too high and/or too deep--Make them pay! ☺ Hit a hard shot down toward their feet.

Make sure you do NOT back up! Many players back up to let a high dink bounce and they miss an excellent offensive put-away shot while putting themselves back on the defense.

A Shallow Dink

If your practice partner hits a dink that falls in the shallow half of the kitchen, step in to the kitchen with ONE foot and then immediately step back out with your paddle up after completing your shot.

A Deep Dink

If their dinks are deep into the kitchen, landing near your feet, then practice volleying them in the air and hitting a drop-volley, which drops across the net into the shallow part of the kitchen.

While people are practicing, the most common feedback I offer is, "Paddle up! Paddle up! After every shot, get your paddle UP!"

It takes some practice, but people start to distinguish when to volley the ball instead of dinking, and when to smack a put-away instead of just returning a volley.

Once we wrap up the drill set, we're back to our circle again. "So, now do you see the difference between a volley and put-away?" I ask.

"Yep, and now I know why it's important to make your dink a good one!" a guy up front says.

"So, the dink is what you start with, it's how you build your point. The volley keeps you in play if the opponent hits the ball hard, and the put-away is how you close out the point, *once you've waited for a good opening."*

"But Prem," another fellow says, "I get it now, and I believe you, I think my game will definitely be better from our practice today, but don't you think it's just kind of *boring* to play a soft, slow game?"

"I guess that depends on your definition of boring," I reply, "and what your goal is in playing. At some point, you have to ask yourself, 'Do I want to just keep beating (or losing to) the same people I always do? Or do I actually want to improve my game?' It's fine to just play for fun, but if you want to win more points or play against better players, then playing Smart Pickleball™ is the way to go.

"Now as for the slow game being boring, let me give you an analogy that might make it a little… should I say… sexier...

"I'd like you to imagine a tiger on the plains of Asia. Dangerous, powerful, and damn good at hunting…right?

"What makes a tiger menacing? Is it menacing because it chases after every potential prey like a dog barking at every car that goes by? No, that's too pedestrian...

"The terrifying thing about a tiger is that its prey *doesn't even know it's there*. It's slow, it's patient, it's calm and it is oh-so-alert. It crouches. It creeps. It's just waaaaaaiiiting for the right moment to make its move and when it does, it will take down its prey, almost instantly in one fell swoop.

"So think of the crouching tiger when you try to play Smart Pickleball™. Every drop shot you hit, you're just the big cat waiting for its opening. Every dink you make is just another sloooow, but oh-so-significant step toward your prey… Does thinking of it that way help make it a little more interesting?" I ask Mr. Boring.

"Definitely!" he replies, no longer so bored at the idea.

"Now, finally, can we all agree that the softer shots in pickleball are not wimpy shots, but *au contraire*, can you see how they fit together to make a formidable, powerful, and winning pickleball game?"

"Yes!"

"Great," I say. "Well, let's see how you do when we take what you've learned out of the drill format and into the game format."

Segment 3: Putting It All Together

"With this drill, we're gonna put it all together—everything we've practiced over the last two days. In a few minutes, I'm going to ask you to go out on the court and play out a few points.

"Before we do, I want to go on the record and tell you something. Is everyone with me? Are you sure? I want to make sure you hear me say this…Ready?

"Now that you're going to be in a game setup, what's going to happen is you're going to start to focus on scoring a point so you can win the drill, and you're going to *forget about everything you've learned over the last two days.*

"Hear that? Now don't let it happen. The only way you can stop it is to consciously make the decision to focus on practicing instead of winning. You're still in the clinic (need I remind you that you paid to play out these next points?), so don't waste your time trying to win. Make the most of this opportunity by consciously deciding to implement the skills you've developed this weekend.

"Got it?"

Then I go on to explain what's going to happen next. This is the only drill where we *don't* have all six people on the court.

The people on the court play out the first four points of a game. The people watching from the sideline are tasked with the job of judging how well the players are implementing what we practiced.

You can read more about it in the drill below.

The Guru's Drill: Play to Practice

Materials

- 4 players
- 2 Smart Pickleball™ observers

Instructions

Start as if in a regular game, but instead of playing to 11 points, you're only going to play to 4 points.

As the first few shots of the game are played, have each observer focus on one team. Then have the observer call out "Good!" or "Short!" based on how deep the serve and return of serve are.

Once the third shot is hit, have them call out "Good!" or "Not a drop shot!" based on the type of shot attempted.

Have them call out "Paddle up, [player name]!" if they see someone's paddle down between shots.

Notice how difficult it can be to stay focused on practicing what you've learned during scored play, but remember it is oh-so-important to be able to actually integrate what you learn in drills.

Once you've played to four points, have the team that *won* sit out, split the teams, and start over. (Having the winning team sit out is extra encouragement to focus on practicing instead of winning and it also gives the people who need the most practice more practice time.)

Advanced Option

Once the observers see that the players are consistently hitting deep serves, deep returns, going for the drop on the third shot, and keeping their paddle up, have one player from each side focus on adding in the "Call the Ball" drill, starting with saying either "Me" or "You" for every shot.

• •

When the time is up, I call everyone back to the group to hear about how it went.

"You were right, Prem," one woman says, "I was determined to practice what you taught us, and still I just fell back into my old patterns."

"It was tricky, but I can already see how different my serves and returns are than they were before. I can't wait to see how I do when I go back to play with people who haven't attended this clinic," says another woman.

"Yes, please keep me posted!" I say.

"Now, we've got some time left to do a few Q & A's before wrapping up. What questions do you have for me?"

Frequently Asked Questions: Part 2

"Prem, do you have any suggestions for what to do when I'm playing with a lefty?" a sandy-haired man named Jorje asks.

Playing As a Left-Right Combination

"Sure," I answer, "I can give you some tips. I hear that question a lot. For those of you who are beginners or have never paid much attention to how playing with or against a lefty changes the dynamics of the game, here's why it matters:

"When you're playing WITH a lefty, you are always going to have either two backhands in the middle or two forehands in the middle. This can sometimes be great, especially if you and your partner both have strong forehands, you'll feel practically invincible as you put away every ball your opponents pop up to the middle.

"Until you finally score a point.

"Because, then, you switch to the other position on the court and suddenly you have two backhands in the middle. If your opponents are playing smart, you'll miss ball after ball because you're both expecting the other person to hit it and nobody has a forehand in the middle with which to make a good shot.

"So how do you figure out who takes the middle shots?

"Communication!

When you're part of a left-right combination, decide at the beginning of the game (or each point) who is going to take the middle shots. Then, have that person take *all* the shots that come to the middle.

"Depending on your relative strengths as players, you should also consider whose backhand is stronger and whose forehand is stronger. Then, depending on whether you have forehands in the middle or backhands in the middle, have the person with the stronger shot take all the balls that come to the middle when you're in that position. Does that make sense?"

"Sure," Jorje says, "but what if the ball is just out of the person's reach?"

"Call it. Ask your partner to take it. When you are part of a left-right combination, it is *even more essential* to make sure to CALL every ball you can."

Now, since you and I have the luxury of communicating through this book, my dear reader, I'm going to delve into a little bit more depth than I have time for in a clinic.

A Tip for Advanced Players

For those of you who really like to analyze the game, here's another tip:

If you are part of a left-right combination and you're hitting a shot that's come to the *middle* between you and your partner, your best bet is to hit the ball *cross-court* to the person in front of your partner.

Why? This draws upon the logic I outlined in describing how to know when to cover the line or cover the middle.

If you are about to hit a shot in the middle of the court, it means you are not covering your line. So if you hit to the person directly opposite you, your line (or what they call the alley in tennis) is wide open for them to hit down.

Now, when you're about to hit that shot in the middle, your partner should be shifted slightly to be covering their line/alley, since they don't NEED to be covering the middle. So, if you hit the ball cross-court to the person in front of your partner, it will be difficult for them to make an offensive shot because two-thirds of the court is covered by you and your partner.

You will have effectively forced them to hit directly to one of you or to make a very difficult cross-court dink. (Even better if you can hit to the person's backhand because it will make it difficult for them to do anything other than just dink the ball back to you.)

Okay, back to our clinic.

"Prem, how about any tips for how to play *against* a right-left combination?" a man near the front asks.

Tips to Play Against a Right-Left Combination

"Aaaah, great question!" I say, "And not one that I hear too often! When your opponents are a left-right combination, this presents a great opportunity for you to take advantage of their indecision as you hit shots right between them that neither of them will hit because they both thought the other person was going to take it. (At this point, if you're like many of us, you'll semi-obnoxiously cheer, 'That's why they say, "Down the middle solves the riddle, baby!" but I don't necessarily recommend saying such things.)'

Hit to the Middle

"When you're playing against a left-right combination, hit to the middle of the two players.

"For a long time when I said, 'Hit to the middle,' people would think I meant to the middle of the court, and (even my wife, Wendy) would aim for the 'T' at the kitchen. But what I really mean is to hit *between* the two players. No matter where they are on the court, centered on each of their halves of the court or one covering the line and one covering the middle, aim for the halfway point between the two players. Got it?

"In most cases, this applies whether they have forehands OR backhands in the middle. Obviously, don't hit the ball high enough that it's in their wheelhouse where they can smack a put-away shot, but if you keep your shots low and slow, the added confusion of who is going to take the shot is a greater advantage to you than the lower-percentage shot of trying to hit to their backhands, where you risk hitting into the higher part of the net or hitting the ball wide."

Slower Balls Are Better Than Faster/Harder Balls

"Another tip: When you're playing against a left-right combination, hit slower balls to increase the odds of your opponents confusing themselves.

"Think about it. A ball that is slow coming and that they have to wait to bounce gives them MUCH more time to get confused about who is going to hit it. A ball that is hard or fast is one they are both likely to just react to and at least one is likely to hit.

"Pretty smart, eh?"

Lob Smart

"If you like to lob and are consistent with it, lob to the *middle* of the *back third* of the court when your opponents have their *backhands* in the middle.

"Like I say though in my section about the lob, you better make sure it's a good one or you're liable to have the ball slammed back down your throat (or at the very least, at your feet) in no time flat.

"Sadly, I think the reason I don't hear it much is because a surprising number of players never even NOTICE when one of their opponents is left-handed (not to mention if *both* of them happen to be).

"Sure, you get to know the local players in your group who are lefties, so you are *kind of* prepared to try not to feed it straight to their wheelhouse. But as you improve your game and play against new and better players, you can't just rely on familiarity and if you're gonna play Smart Pickleball™, you *gotta* take factors like that into account.

"So, have a mental checklist you go through at the beginning of EVERY match, and make sure the first question you ask yourself is, 'Is my partner or either of my opponents left-handed?'

"You just can't play a smart game of pickleball if you're not clear when you're hitting to your opponent's forehand and when you're hitting to their backhand, and you can't know THAT unless you know whether they are a lefty or a righty. (Not counting the rare cases of players who successfully switch the paddle between both hands.) Make sense?"

People are really thinking now...

Then someone else asks, "Prem, what about that thing people do sometimes where they are always switching from the odd court to the even or vice versa?"

Playing Switch-a-Roo

"I know what you mean," I say. "How many of you know what she means?"

A few people raise their hands.

"I don't have another word for it other than 'playing switch-a-roo.' For those of you who aren't familiar with it, there is no rule about where the partner of the server or receiver can stand. So, say you're a right-left combination and you're stuck with backhands in the middle. Rather than playing that way the whole point, some teams will have the right-handed person serve or return the serve and have the lefty stand *outside* the court to their right."

Here are some diagrams to show you what I mean.

Switch-a-roo Shifting After Serve

Switch-a-roo Shifting After Return of Serve

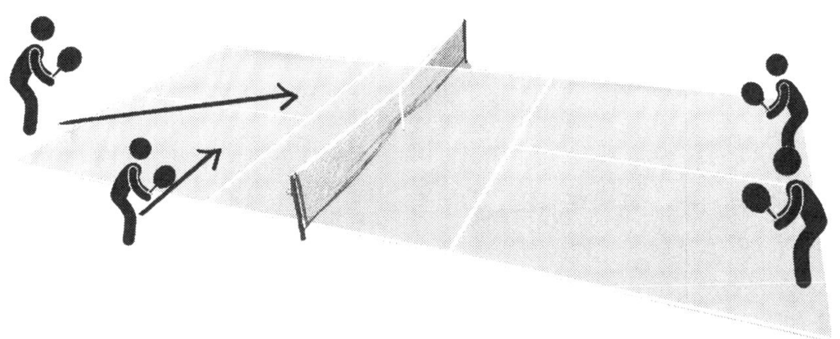

"If you and your partner play dramatically better in a particular configuration (usually forehands in the middle for a left-right combination) you may opt to *always* stay in that configuration.

"This can get VERY confusing because you must still make sure that the correct person is serving and receiving from the correct position.

"Keeping track of the score, and whose serve it is, is hard enough for most players, let alone figuring it out when you're standing on the wrong sides of the court!

"This is an advanced strategy that is often more confusing than it is effective, however at top levels, it is regularly used to a good advantage for both left-right combinations as well as combinations where one player is perceived as being considerably stronger than the other.

"Other questions?" I ask.

One woman says, "Prem, I'm pretty new to the game. I know you have your signature paddle for sale. I tried it out today at lunch and really liked it, but I just bought a new paddle a couple months ago. Can you tell me a little more about how to pick a good paddle and what sets yours apart?"

"An opportunity to talk about why I love my signature paddle? How could I resist?" I tease. "But first I'll start out with some generalities.

"First of all, how many of you know that Wilson has entered the market with their own pickleball paddle?"

About a quarter of the group raise their hand.

"If you ask me, that's a sure sign that the sport is on the rise!"

How to Pick the Right Paddle So It Helps (Instead of Hurts) Your Game

"Now, If you've been playing pickleball for any length of time, you've probably asked yourself three questions:

- Should I buy a new pickleball paddle?
- What kind of paddle should I buy?
- With so many options, how do I know which one is right for me?

"Without going into a comprehensive analysis of the pros and cons of every pickleball paddle on the market, I'll give you some guidelines to choose a paddle that works for you and your game in particular. First let's talk about weight."

Weight

"Pickleball paddles generally range in weight from 6.8 oz (about the weight of a softball) to 14 oz (almost the weight of a can of green beans).

"The advantage of a lighter paddle is that it is easier to maneuver (especially up at the net during quick volleys).

"Anybody know the disadvantage of a paddle that is too light?"

A man with a wrap on his forearm yells out, "It gives you tennis elbow like I got!"

"Exactly. You experience more of the impact/vibration in your arm and elbow because there is less mass to counteract the ball. Of course, this is much less in pickleball compared to tennis, for example, but it can make quite a difference, as our injured friend here can attest.

"The heavier your paddle, the more 'oomph' it adds to your slams and hard shots, but the more strength it takes to control it on the softer shots."

The Bottom Line

"If you are a current or former table tennis player, or you're accustomed to using your wrist to execute many of your shots, you'll probably prefer a light- to medium-weight paddle.

"If you are a current or former tennis player, you may prefer a heavier paddle because you're accustomed to the weight of your tennis racket in your hand."

"Now let's talk about length. I saw one of you is playing with an extra-long paddle. I was one of the first to buy one and Wendy calls it 'the fly swatter.'"

Length

"The regulations for the dimensions of a pickleball paddle are based on the total area, or the length times the widest width. Most paddles add length to the face by shortening the length of the handle, keeping the total length and width the same. This is true for most wide-body and oversize paddles. The 'fly swatter style' paddle opts for a much narrower face in order to add an extra inch or so of length.

"There are two main advantages of a longer paddle: Number one, it gives you that much more of a reach to volley balls without stepping into the kitchen, and number two, you get a little extra speed because of the added distance from the center of rotation when you hit the ball.

"On the other hand, that extra distance also makes the paddle head feel slightly heavier and less maneuverable at the net."

The Bottom Line

"I suggest that you stick to a regular, wide-body or oversize paddle head, but don't bother with the extra-long paddles unless you are a particularly advanced racket-sport player who almost ALWAYS hits the sweet-spot on your paddle and doesn't need much extra width.

"Then, we're on to the big question of power versus control."

Power vs. Control

"Some paddles (graphite- or cork-centered, or fiberglass-faced paddles) will give you lots of 'pop' for very little effort. This is great for hitting the ball over the net from the back of the court just by sticking your paddle in front of it, whether you're hitting a half-volley drop shot to come up to the net, or whether you tend to play your entire game from the baseline. (Not a strategy I recommend, obviously.) But the disadvantage of a paddle with so much pop is that it's harder to control the ball.

"The very same attributes that launch the ball from the back of the court can work against you when you are at the net. When you are dinking at the net, paddles that provide a lot of pop will often make your dinks go higher or deeper than other paddles, which as you know by now, is *not* a good thing.

"Up at the net, if you stick that same paddle in front of the ball, it will make the ball fly much higher/further than you hope, reminding you what it feels like to 'leave your partner hung out to dry' as your opponent smashes the ball at their feet."

"That said, occasionally the added speed off the paddle face makes it harder for some opponents to return volleys."

The Bottom Line

"If you're a tournament player and/or you're working on integrating the dink into your game, I suggest you opt for control rather than power with a composite paddle. If you tend to stay at the back of the court or want maximum speed with minimum effort, a paddle with more power might be right for you.

"If you are an avid singles player, then definitely go for a paddle with more power, since singles is less dependent on dinks or drop shots. Is that helpful?"

I get many head nods.

"Anything else?" I ask.

"What about the color of the paddle, Prem? I notice it's sometimes easy to lose the ball in a yellow paddle. Do you recommend getting yellow for that reason?"

Color

"It sure is easy to lose a ball in a yellow shirt or paddle! I don't have a lot to say on this, but unless and until the USAPA makes yellow paddles and/or shirts illegal, it is still a substantial advantage to play with a yellow paddle. It really does make it that much harder for your opponent to see the ball as it comes off your paddle."

The Bottom Line

"I have a yellow paddle, I also have other color paddles. Whether or not you decide to use the color advantage is, of course, your choice. If you don't, you might just decide to get a paddle to match your every outfit, and you wouldn't be the first pickleball player to do so. (Really!)"

"And in case it needs to be said, playing Smart Pickleball™ is obviously going to be much more of an advantage than buying a yellow paddle…" I say, wryly.

"The main thing I'd say to you is: Don't stress about buying a paddle. If you're someone who isn't very particular or happens to be very lucky, a random paddle you buy off the internet could last you a decade. But, if you're like most avid players, your preferences and tastes will change as your game develops and evolves. Start with a cheaper or used paddle and move your way up the ladder as you find what you like.

"Now, before we go I can't pass up the opportunity for some shameless self-promotion."

"I've put my signature on the pickleball paddle that offers the best balance of power and control. In the past six years, I've bought my-wife-won't-even-let-me-say-how-many paddles.

"My signature paddle is manufactured by Pro-Lite and has a graphite core with a matte finish. It has enough weight to give some ka-bang to an overhead, without being too heavy at the net, and it has a slightly longer handle to take advantage of a good wrist flick.

"So, if you want to stop shopping around and you're ready to get a fantastic all-around paddle built to last and endorsed by someone you trust, get The Pickleball Guru signature paddle today. You'll be glad you did."

You can order online by going to: www.PickleballGuru.com/paddle

I often sell several paddles in a clinic, and I encourage people to try out my tester. If you have a paddle you want to try out, here are some tips for how to test it.

The Guru's Drill: For Testing a Paddle

Control

Stand at the no-volley line, and have someone hit the ball hard at you. Just try to take the pace off the ball by holding the paddle firmly and trying to drop the ball right over the net. Notice how many of your shots fall into the kitchen or how far past the kitchen line they go.

Pop

Off the Half-Volley

Have someone hit an overhead hard at you, while you are in the back of the court. Just stick your paddle out firmly to block the ball as it comes up off the bounce and notice how often the ball goes back over the net, or whether it falls short.

Off the Lob

Practice hitting overheads and pay attention to the power that the paddle adds (or doesn't add) to your shot.

Maneuverability

Volley back and forth with someone at the net, alternating forehands and backhands. Practice bringing your paddle back to the ready position after each shot. Notice how easy it is to maneuver the paddle, notice any strain in your wrist, forearm, or shoulder.

Solutions for the Emotional Aspects

In my travels and via my website, I often get questions about the emotional side of pickleball.

"Prem, do you have any suggestions for how to get rid of the butterflies when I play in a tournament?"

"Prem, it seems silly, but I swear, ever since my JV coach told me I would never be any good at sports, I have stopped believing I can win—even when I play teams that I KNOW I should beat..."

"Prem, I get so close to winning, and then I let up and end up losing the game... Help!"

No matter how many hours we put into drilling and practicing, when we get in a competitive situation, it's a different ball game, so to speak. Whether you're playing in a tournament or just find yourself matched against the best team in your group, it's easy to crumble when the pressure is on.

The emotional side of sports can have a lot to do with whether you win or lose a game. A bad call, repeated net shots, or miscommunication between you and your partner can cause any team to perform worse than their potential.

Here are some of the best (if somewhat bizarre) solutions I have come across to address the nebulous emotional aspects of competitive pickleball.

Bach Rescue Remedy

The best cure that my wife and I have found for the inevitable pre-tournament jitters is called Bach Rescue Remedy. It is available at most health food stores, Sprout's Markets, Whole Foods, Henry's Markets, etc., for about $12. We like the spray, although there are lozenges and tinctures as well. Don't ask me why it works, but most of the time, it just does.

HeartMath

This is the one I know the least about and have the least experience with, but it came into my awareness recently and I think for some of you, it might be just the right thing. Corporations such as Hewlett-Packard, Motorola, and all four branches of the U.S. military, are now using HeartMath techniques to teach employees how to become more mentally and emotionally balanced, and provide for individual and organizational transformation. Educators have found that school children can better manage their behavior, and improve their ability to absorb academic information by using the techniques.

Who knows what it will do for your pickleball game. For a brief explanation of what HeartMath is and how to use the "Freeze Frame" technique, see the description of the PBS special on the topic at: http://www.pbs.org/bodyandsoul/203/heartmath.htm.

Emotional Freedom Technique (EFT)

Now this is the one that will probably seem a little bizarre at first, but again, I'm including it here because I have seen it work wonders for myself and others. It's called Emotional Freedom Technique, or EFT. Sometimes it's also called Tapping because it consists of tapping on various acupressure spots on the face and torso. (Hey, if they can perform painless surgery in China using a little acupuncture, it's got to be more powerful than most of us know.)

In one study conducted at Oregon State University, there was a 38% difference between the basketball free-throw performance of a group who used this technique over a placebo group.

There aren't many EFT resources out yet for pickleball, but there are plenty on its effectiveness in other sports.

For a few videos that may pique your interest and convince you to find out more about EFT, go to www.ThePickleballGuru.com/EFT – And most importantly, don't just read about it, but actually TRY IT and USE IT on a regular basis. It won't just change your pickleball game, it can change your life.

With that, let me bring your attention back to our clinic now.

"Well, friends, our time together is coming to an end. I have one more thing I'd like to remind you of, which will also cover my tail so that you aren't blaming me and telling anyone, 'Oh this guy messed up my game!'" I quip.

"I want you to think about improving your level of play like accelerating a car. So here's my question for you: How many of you have driven a stick-shift car?"

Most of the hands go up.

"Good, looks like most of you have. So what do you do when you're accelerating, for example, from first gear to second gear? What exactly do you do?"

Someone calls out, "Press the clutch, release the accelerator, shift to second gear, and then accelerate and release the clutch."

"And when you press the clutch, what do you do?"

They're looking a little unsure. "We shift from first to second!"

"Yes, but what happens between first and second? There's a phase between first and second, what is it?"

"Oh! We go through neutral!" a woman calls out excitedly from the right.

"Yes! You go through neutral. For that moment of time, you are actually decelerating. And yet, it's essential because you could never go as fast in first as you can in second, right?

"It's the same thing with your game. Since attending this clinic, you've found out where second gear is and you're ready to accelerate. But in order to actually get there and play better, you're going to go through a period of deceleration.

"Don't get focused on it. If you got distracted with disappointment that the car was slowing down once you put the clutch in, you'd lose the opening to speed up. While you're decelerating, you might set yourself up in a bad way because you tried for a new shot. You might lose 11-0 to a team you wouldn't normally have lost to. You might undermine your reputation as a hard-hitter by trying out some soft shots.

"Who cares? Just decide what you want to practice and practice it.

"You're trying to implement new information and your body has to get used to it. As long as you're practicing what you learned this weekend, you're gassing up and you *will* re-accelerate through the deceleration. Be patient, trust your learning, and your game will only improve with time.

"Make sense?" I ask.

I get fervent nods of confirmation.

"So on that note, I'd like you all to lift up your right hand…"

I demonstrate and get most of the group responding.

"Raise it high, now I want you to stretch your arm out to the right… Yep, That's right…And now…I want you to use that hand to give the person next to you a pat on the back and say, "Well done, nice work!'"

I get a lot of smiles, some enthusiastic cheers, and many shouts of, "Thanks, so much, Prem!"

It's been another full, rewarding weekend of teaching Smart Pickleball™. Of course, that's not where my work ends. I've got more private lessons lined up and I'd be delighted to have you sit it on them with me, but first, I'm off for a much-needed lunch break...

Private Lesson #2

Coming back to the courts after a tasty Thai lunch with a few students, I find my next group already gathered around my ball hopper. They're all ladies. Two of them, Jean and Devi, were in the clinic with me, two were not. One of the women from the clinic is the local USAPA Ambassador, Jean, who put in a lot of time and energy to make my clinic happen.

It always amazes me to see how much dedication people like Jean have to their volunteer positions, and it warms my heart when I find out how satisfied they were to bring me to their location.

"Oh, Prem, the clinic was such a hit! A group of us went out to lunch together and people were so enthusiastic!" Jean gushes. "They can't wait to get out and play with their regular groups."

"Wow, sounds like we missed out on something good," says Nancy, a brown-haired athletic type with a pony tail, to Veronica, the other woman who was not at the clinic.

"Don't worry, ladies, there's always next time," I offer. "And you'll learn a lot in our time together today. Speaking of which, let's get started. Did you have an idea of what you want to work on today?"

"Well, I think I'd like to work on my net game," says Veronica, a little timidly. Perhaps she knows how much we worked on the net game during the clinic. In any case, it really doesn't make any difference to me. Somehow I always manage to find ways to engage everyone in a small group lesson, as this quote from one of my students speaks to.

> *"After watching Prem play at the local courts we were impressed with his style of play, his passion to help people and the way he conducted himself on the court. I was not sure how a lesson with myself and my wife would go as we are at different levels of play. Turned out awesome!! The Pickleball Guru identified our weak points and got us both doing drills together that helped us work out our issues. He has a good eye for picking out details, the good and the bad, and is quick to use positive reinforcement when you do things right. We will definitely be taking another lesson before we head home to Vancouver Island and only wish we had better access to his expertise for the rest of the year."*
>
> – Marc Somner | Vancouver Island, BC

Back to our lesson, though.

"There are a few players at our club who always hit the ball with a lot of spin and no matter what I do, my return seems to go into the net. I'd like to find out how to hit those shots better," Jean says.

"Sure. No problem, we can work on both of those," I answer. "How about you, Nancy? Devi?"

"Well, I feel a little stuck. I love playing with the gals I usually play with, but we're all at about the same level and if anything, I'm one of the stronger players, and it just doesn't challenge me like I think I need. There's another group of lady players who is at a little higher level than we are, but they never seem to want to play with us. I'd like you to help me find the weakness in my game so that I'm at a level where it would be reasonable for me to go and play with them," replies Nancy.

"Ahhh, I see," I respond. "We can certainly start off with a couple practice points so I can see how you play, and I'm sure I'll be able to give you some pointers."

"And, me," Devi begins, "well, I guess I'm a little like Jean, except it's not so much the spin that throws me off as when people, especially some of the men, really whale on the ball and hit it so hard at the net. So I guess I'd like to work on my net play, too. But, also, I learned to play here on the outdoor courts but we are heading up north to visit our kids this winter and we'll be playing indoors. I'd love it if you could give us some tips on playing indoor versus outdoor."

"Mm-hmm, of course...Okay, ladies, well it sounds like we have our work cut out for us. We're gonna start out playing just a couple points out so I can see how you play, and then we'll get started with the drills, sound good?"

They all nod.

"All right, off you go!"

They miss their first couple shots, but I can tell it's probably just nerves. As friendly as I can be, and as non-judgmental as I am, when someone who's known as "The Pickleball Guru" is in the process of evaluating or critiquing your pickleball game, people tend to get a little jumpy.

"No pressure, ladies, forget I'm even here, just pretend it's a usual day at the pickleball courts," I call out.

In a matter of minutes they are engrossed in their play and I've seen enough to know what we need to work on so I call them together at the net.

"Okay, the first thing I want to work on, which will help you two especially, Devi and Veronica, is to work on staying up to the line."

"Really?" Devi asks. "I thought I *was* up at the line."

(Do you start to see, dear reader, how much of my work with students is on helping them *actually* do what they mistakenly believe they are *already* doing?)

"Well, let me say this. You are all pretty good about coming up toward the kitchen line to play the point, but between the four of you, you fall prey to what I call 'The two lies you tell yourself when you're at the line.'

"Hmmm, okay..." Devi answers, dubiously.

The Two Lies You Tell Yourself When You're at The Line

"The first lie people tell themselves, is that they are 'at the line' if they are within about two feet of it. Now, when I say 'at the line' I mean you better have your feet about two *inches* from the line."

Lie #1: I am "at the line" if I am within two feet of the line.

"Really?" Devi asks again. "But won't we make lots of foot faults if we're that close to the line?"

"Well, that's the trick," I say. "You need to always know where you are in relationship to the line, and plant your feet right behind it, so that you *know* that the only time you're going to step forward is to take a ball off the bounce, which is, of course, when it's perfectly legal to step over the line.

"It's absolutely something you need to drill on so that you don't get called on foot faults, or worse, NOT get called on them, marvel at the excellent shots you're hitting, and then find out after the fact that they weren't actually as legal as you thought.

"We'll practice more in a minute, but first I want to tell you about the other lie. The second lie people tell themselves is that getting up to the line at all is the same as staying at the line. Veronica, this is what you can work on. You see you did a great job of coming right up to the back of the line. But two shots later, you had backed up so you were a good two or three feet from the kitchen."

Lie #2: Getting up to the line at all is the same as staying at the line.

"I always tell my students, never, ever, *ever* back up from the line to take a ball. Once you back up, it's hard to come back, and it's more likely your opponent will just keep hitting them at your feet to push you back from the line, shot by shot.

"So now I want you all up here at the kitchen, and I want you to dink and volley like you would during the game, but every time you back up from the line, I'm going to call you on it. Take your positions please."

Already, Devi is about a foot farther back from the line than the rest of them.

"Devi, look at your feet. How far are your toes from the line?" I ask.

"Hmmm, maybe about ten inches?" So she shuffles her feet about four inches closer.

"Deeeeeviiiii, *now* how far are your toes from the line?" I ask again.

"You mean you want me closer than *this*?" she asks, more than a little surprised.

The other ladies chuckle a bit.

"Take a look at Nancy's toes. Remember I said two inches? By two inches, I meant *two inches*. Now move up closer again," I tell her.

She sighs, but finally gets her feet in position.

"Okay, great. I know it's gonna feel awkward at first, but for right now, while we hit, I want you to focus on hitting the ball and always leaving one foot right where it is right now. If you need to take the ball off the bounce, step into the kitchen with one foot. Leave the other foot exactly where it is so that you can come back to the same position, knowing that it is legal because you are behind the line.

"Okay, ladies, start dinking. If it's a high dink, volley it. If it's a high ball, put it away."

Devi does alright staying near the line.

"Veroooonicaaaaa… you're backing uuuuup... What did I tell you? Don't back up! Get back up to that line, missy!" I say encouragingly.

And back up to the line she goes.

A few minutes later she pauses to say, "Prem, every time you tell me I'm backing up, it's because I felt like I had to back up to get the ball because it was deep. If I'm not supposed to back up, how am I supposed to get those balls?" she asks.

"Sure," I answer. "Good question. Instead of stepping back, take the ball in the air. You're not the only person to think that if you are standing at the kitchen line and the ball is bouncing at or near your feet, your HAVE to back up to take it off the bounce. In fact, this is just because you are taking the ball later than you should be. If the ball is going to bounce at your feet, then the trajectory is such that you probably could have taken it in the air, so reach down and out if necessary, and try to hit that ball before it bounces."

The diagram below is illustrative of what I demonstrate.

Hit the Ball in the Air Instead of Waiting Until It Bounces

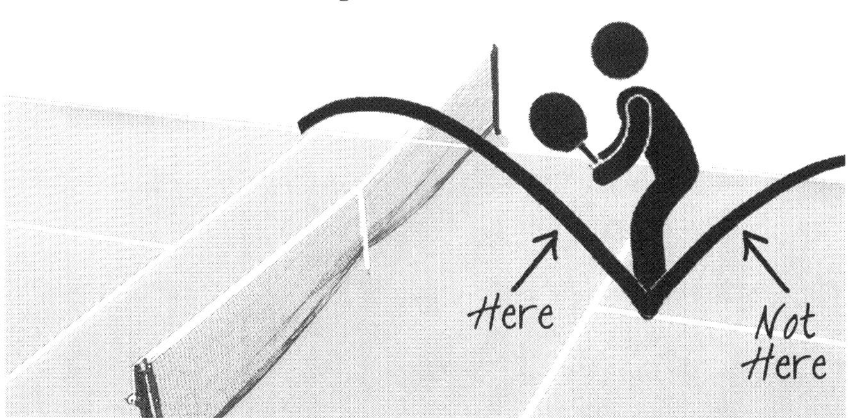

Veronica tries this for the next few shots and shortly gets the hang of it.

We go on drilling for about twenty minutes. It's the constant feedback each time they get out of position that will remind them to stay in position when they are in a game. After the drills, I ask them to play out a couple points, applying what they practiced, and in no time at all they are all being much more consistent.

Here's a quote from one of my students who participated in a private lesson with drills very similar to the one I am describing here.

"Since I am new to the sport I was reluctant to take a class but I am glad I did. Your teaching style is relaxed and I was comfortable learning new things. The drills come back to me while I play now. ... I can hear your voice "Missy, get back to that line!" Another benefit of your class is that I found a partner to play with in the recent tournament...Two bronze medals! Thank you, Prem!"

— Sandy Seigen | Fallbrook, CA

How to Play Against Someone Who Spins the Ball

"Okay, next, let's return to Jean's question about how to play against someone who is hitting the ball with a lot of spin. My tips here are very similar to my secret for hitting many other shots.

Secret #1: Wait until the ball is past the top of the arch and almost to the second bounce.

This is similar to the strategy I talk about regarding how to hit a good drop shot.

In fact, I'm even going to use the same rough diagram.

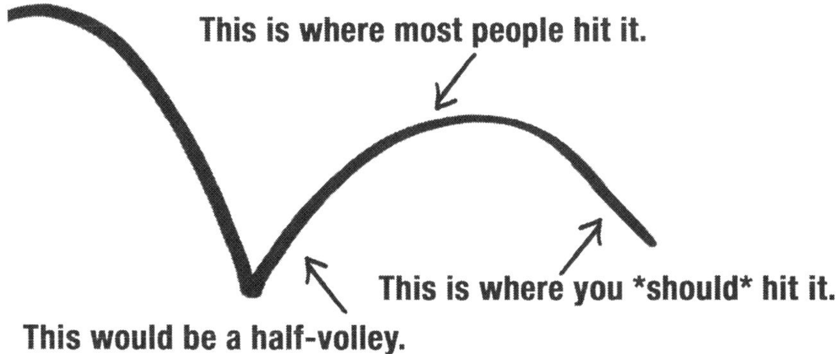

"If you hit the ball in the course of its arch between the first two arrows, it will still have a strong spin on it, and it is likely to fly wildly out of your control. But as the ball reaches the apex of the bounce, the spin has drastically diminished and you'll have a MUCH better chance of hitting a decent shot back. Also, the longer you wait (the closer you take it to the third arrow) the more control you will have over your shot. Make sense?"

"I believe you, but I'll have to try it for myself," Jean says.

"Of course, let me give you one more pointer and then we'll practice," I answer.

"The second way you can get more control of a spinning ball is to anticipate that it's going to bounce funny. You can actually predict whether it's going to bounce lower or higher than usual based on the person's paddle motion as they hit the ball."

Secret #2: Expect the Ball to Bounce Higher or Lower Based on How They Hit It

"You don't need to know a LOT about how they hit their topspin shot or their slice shot, but you should know what to expect from the ball based on how they hit it.

"In many cases, your opponent is back in no-man's land or all the way at the back of the court so it's easy to get a perspective on their overall motion. (There's a good chance of this because tennis players are often the ones using a lot of spin, and most of them haven't been enlightened as to the value of getting up to the line.)

"Watch the motion of their paddle as they hit the ball, is it from high to low or low to high?"

I demonstrate a slice shot and ask Jean, "What did you see my paddle do when I hit the ball?"

"It went from high to low," she answers.

"Right you are. Now watch this one."

I show her a top-spin shot. "What happened there?" I ask.

"Low to high." I look around at the others. "Did everyone see that?"

They nod their heads yes.

Below are some diagrams to show you what I mean. You can watch a video where I explain a little more about the spin at: www.PickleballGuru.com/spin

---

If they hit a top-spin shot, where their paddle moves from low to high over the ball, then you can expect the ball to bounce higher than normal.

Top Spin = Low to High = Ball Bounces Higher

If they move their paddle from high to low and hit the ball at a downward and cross-the-body angle, then they are hitting a slice shot, and the ball is likely to bounce lower than normal.

Slice = High to Low = Ball Bounces Lower

"Now, I want to remind you, don't pay attention to where the paddle ends up *after* the shot, just watch the motion of the paddle *as they hit* the ball.

"Just having that extra half-second heads-up to know whether to expect the ball to bounce lower or higher than normal, and then waiting that next extra half second until the ball reaches (at least) the top of the arch, will improve eighty percent of the shots you hit against someone who spins the ball."

So I send the four ladies off to one side of the net and practice hitting some spin-y shots to each of them. The first couple go into the net, so I offer "Wait a little longer before you hit it," or "Did you see how that was higher than you were expecting?" and they catch on pretty quickly.

"Okay, that's something I'm not gonna spend too much more time on today because you get the picture and you can practice in everyday play.

"Before we wrap up, I want to come back to Nancy's question about what she needs to do to play with the better players. Now, Nancy, having seen you play and hit the ball in our drills here, I can say you're playing *great*."

"Thanks, Prem," she answers.

"And I agree," I continue, "the best way for you to keep improving is to play with better players. It forces you to play at the top of your ability, makes you pay for your mistakes, and puts you on the fast-track to a higher skill level.

"So the tips I have for you are not about improving your play, but I want to talk a little bit about etiquette and how you can politely find a way into that higher level group. Perhaps you've seen my newsletter article on this topic, it's called 'How to Get to Play with Better Players and Make Sure You're NOT That Person Everyone Hates Playing With.' Have you seen it?"

None of them have, so I give them a summary of the following points.

Pickleball Etiquette: How to Get to Play with Better Players and Make Sure You're NOT That Person Everyone Hates Playing With

When You Want to Join Players Who Are STRONGER Than You...

- Politely ask if they mind you joining, and also give them an out. For example, *"Do you all mind if I get a game in with you or would you rather just play on your own?"*
- When you ask, make sure it's at the beginning or end of the day, when they are warming up or cooling down. DON'T go

when they are in the midst of a streak of higher-level play.

- If you do approach them in the midst of higher-level play, ask, *"Hey, do you mind if I get a game in with you all before you quit today?"* so that they can continue playing another few games, but will hopefully commit to playing with you before the day is over.
- If they do play a few games with you at the beginning of the day, be conscientious about giving them a chance to play with other higher-level players. Let them KNOW that you're being conscientious, so that they will be more likely to want to play with you again in the future. You might say, *"Hey, I see you can get a good game in against those guys, I'll sit this one out and maybe we can play again later if you have a chance."*
- If you ask a stronger player to join a game with you, HIT TO THEM! Especially in a recreational game, no one likes to sit on a court watching their partner hit all the balls. The higher level player is doing you a favor by playing with you, so hit the ball to them at *least* half the time. It will make you a better player, make it more fun for them, and make it more likely that they will play with you again next time.
- Don't be obnoxious if you beat a stronger player in recreational play. We all play our best when we play with better players. When we play with weaker players, it can be challenging to stay focused, so remember that they may not be playing at the top of their game. (Or, if your opponents have read this book, they may be focusing on improving their own shots, rather than on winning.)
- If they give you feedback on your game, have an open mind and be appreciative of them taking the time to play and help you.

While we're on the topic, I also want to address those higher level players who may sometimes get approached by newer players. It's easy to think that playing with lower level players keeps you from having to play at the top of your ability, keeps you from paying for your mistakes, and keeps you from improving your skill level as quickly. But it doesn't have to be that way. Here are some mental games you can play with the scoring against any level opponents, to stay engaged in the game.

Mental Games You Can Play with the Scoring

Build Yourself a Handicap, Then Come Back for the Win

This is an especially good one to use when you are playing with lower-skilled players. The idea is to be risky at the beginning, go for the tricky serves, go for the corner lines, take the shots that you don't usually make, and let the other team get ahead. Then, once they get to 6 or 8 (or even 9!) points, try going into a more conservative, consistent, reliable mode of play. This way, you'll get a little practice on your risky shots, while also developing confidence that you can play smart and safe when you need to.

Don't Give an Inch

If you're playing against players who are similar to your level, decide that you are going to try for a shut-out — that is, rather than making your goal to just win the game, make your goal not to let them get a single point. If they end up getting 4, then next game, see if you can reduce it to 3.

Pretend the Score Is Different Than It Is

This seems silly, but for some people, including my wife, it sometimes seems to work. If you know that you have a tendency to let up when you are winning 9-4, do this: Every time the score is called, repeat to yourself the opposite score (so pretend you are down 4-9) or maybe even 0-0. Get to know what vantage point is most motivating for you personally, and pretend that that is where you are—even when you're not.

Another thing I am constantly reminding people of is that everyone's gotta start from somewhere, and even the best players in the world were beginners at one point.

The culture of pickleball has always been very welcoming and inclusive of new players, but as you become more intent on improving your game, you DON'T always want to play with less-experienced players. So the question is: As a better player, how do you "remember your roots" and play with lower-level players, and when is it fair to ask them to step aside so you can get higher-level play?

When You Agree to Join Players Who Are WEAKER Than You...

- Remember, someone took you under their wing when you first started playing, so pay it forward and make a point to regularly play with players who are weaker than you. Perhaps you regularly play a warmup game with them, or once a week you decide to dedicate the last half of your play to playing with them. Not only does it build community, it also helps raise the general level of play.
- If players ask to play with you, and you opt to play a higher-level game, let them know when you WOULD be willing to play, perhaps later in the day, or later in the week.
- When you do play, let them know in advance how long you're planning to play. You might say, "I'd love to play with you all for a game or two, but then I'd like to get in with those other players."
- Don't be patronizing—or overly aggressive. Instead of focusing on who wins or loses, find a way to make it challenging for yourself. Pick a shot you want to improve

upon and focus on hitting that shot. Or, try to reduce your number of unforced errors. Focus on keeping the ball in play rather than slamming every put-away shot.

- If you notice something they could be doing better, give them feedback on one aspect of their game during the play. Giving them too many pointers can overwhelm them. Plus, they're probably already a little nervous about playing with or against you, so don't be too critical. After the game, you could ask them if they want some more information or an additional pointer.
- "Now, I'd like to return to Devi's question about how to play indoor conditions versus outdoor conditions. First, I'll review some of the main tips for playing outdoors, and then I'll talk about playing indoors, okay?"
- More nods.

How to Play the Conditions: Indoor & Outdoor Play

Whether you've been freezing your *derrière* off all winter and are heading outside to enjoy the beautiful weather or you're a "poor soul" like me who is suddenly facing hotter temps down in the sunshine states, thousands of players go back and forth between indoor and outdoor play throughout the year.

The basics of the game are the same, of course. But let's knock out the obvious differences:

- When you're playing outdoors, you're dealing with sun and wind which can each have a major impact on the outcome of a game.
- Indoors, you've got a variety of playing surfaces, which often have dead spots, you've got a ceiling to take into account, and walls to smack your paddle up against on a serve or deep return of serve. (Grrrr, isn't it a pain?!)

- Echos and overall sound level can also be an issue for many players, most commonly when playing indoors.
- More often indoors, but sometimes outdoors as well, you have multi-use courts with multiple lines in multiple colors.
- And, of course, at most venues (but not everywhere!) they play with a completely different ball indoors than out.

So how do you make the most of each playing environment?

I'm not going to tell you the obvious things like wear sunscreen, a hat, sunglasses, good court shoes and drink plenty of water when you go outside from indoor play, or to take a step *away* from the wall to hit your serve or return of serve when you're playing indoors.

(Did you notice how I slipped that in, and managed to remind you about those things, without actually telling you? Always thinking two steps ahead in pickleball and in life, I am...!) ☺

But seriously. I've got much better stuff in store for you, so read on.

How to Play the Outdoor Environment

For our purposes, I'm assuming that if you're playing outdoors, you are playing with one of the Singapore balls such as the Dura ball or Onix. These balls are harder than the Jugs ball, which is typically used indoors. They have smaller holes, and they weigh about an ounce more.

I have actually played pickleball outdoors on a clay tennis court (with a Jugs ball) but again, for our purposes, I'm going to assume that if you're playing outdoors it's on a concrete or asphalt court.

The most important things to know and remember about playing outdoors compared to indoors.

- The ball moves much faster (because it's heavier and has less air resistance due to the smaller holes)

- The ball bounces lower (because it's heavier and harder)

So what does that mean for you?

- You don't have as much time to make your shots, so be especially alert and ready to react faster than usual.
- Wait 'til the ball goes past the top of the arc to hit a ball off the bounce. This is always a good idea but particularly coming from indoor play to outdoors, it can help you recoup a bit of that lost time and get better control of the ball.
- And if you *really* want to play better, when the ball doesn't bounce as high, you're just gonna have to bend those knees a little bit. I know, I know... I'd say nine out of ten times when I miss a shot it's because I didn't bend my knees... We all get lazy sometimes, but bending those knees can make all the difference.

How to Play the Sun

Here's my big tip, ready?

Don't look into the sun.

It might seem obvious, but really. Just don't do it. Instead, turn around and position yourself to be ready to hit the ball off the bounce. Or, better yet, make an agreement with your partner that THEY will take those balls, since they generally have a much better line of sight on the ball because they have a different angle when you are looking into the sun. Then, when it's gonna be lost in the sun, call "Switch!" and let them take the shot.

(Meanwhile, I *can't* say that hitting the ball so *your opponents* have to look into the sun isn't an effective strategy. But I would definitely caution you that the lob shot is much less reliable (and therefore less effective) outdoors than in. Rather than playing "dirty" and trying to make your opponents look at the sun (which is just plain nasty in recreational play) I'm always advocating for you to play smart.

How to Play the Wind

You *must* compensate for the wind. My wife, Wendy, wondered if this wouldn't be too obvious, but I can't tell you how many people I see play exactly the same in the wind as without it.

If you're playing into the wind, you have to hit your serve three to five times harder than you would otherwise. And if it's at your back, just give it a light touch. No matter what, account for drift—to the left or right, closer to you, farther away—because it IS gonna move.

That's why it's even more important to keep your eye on the ball when you're playing in the wind. Too often, it's not where you thought it was going to be. Sometimes, there's just nothing you can do, but most of the time, simply making a concerted effort NOT to go for those put-away shots, and to just keep the ball in play, will save the day.

I can't say it enough, but really: Winning a point in pickleball is eighty percent about not screwing up by hitting the ball into the net or out of bounds.

Much like my tips on transitioning from indoor to outdoor, here are some things to think about when playing indoors.

How to Play the Indoor Environment

Between shiny floors, florescent lights, and various wall colors, just being able to SEE the ball on an indoor court is usually the biggest challenge.

- Get a high-contrast ball: I played at a place on Vancouver Island where they dyed the balls dark green, almost black, just to be able to see them against light beige walls. I've heard that recently a variety of different colored Jugs balls are now available.
- Get ready for the ball to slide and skid. Without the gritty surface of most outdoor courts, the ball has a tendency to

travel much further horizontally on a bounce on an indoor court.

- Indoors, a put-away is never a put-away and a winning shot is sometimes just one more decent shot in an incredibly long rally. It's just the way it is. On average, indoor rallies last much, much longer than outdoors. Because the ball is moving slower and the bounce is higher, your opponent has more time to recover and return your "put-away" shot. So don't be over-confident. Always be ready for the next shot, and don't count your chickens before they hatch. Because, honestly, who HASN'T found themselves standing there, in awe of the glorious shot they just hit, only to be shocked that their opponent not only returned it but won the point?
- "All right, ladies," I say, returning to our lesson. "I've worked you pretty hard today but you've done great. Please send me an email in a few days and let me know how our time together has impacted your play, okay?"

"Thanks SO much, Prem, this was great!" Veronica says.

I give hugs, wave goodbye, and am on my way back to the casita someone has generously offered me to take a shower, grab some dinner, and, eventually, fall into bed.

Day 3: A Day of Private Lessons

Typically, I try not to schedule private lessons for the same day as the clinic, but it happens from time to time. Sometimes I'll schedule a day off after the clinic, before diving in to a few full days of teaching three to five lessons a day.

For the purposes of this book, I think I can convey everything else I want to share with you in the context of a couple more lessons.

Private Lesson #3

We're out on the courts bright and early for an 8 a.m. lesson. The air is cool, the sun is shining, and it's a good day to be alive, let alone out on a pickleball court.

My students for this lesson happen to be four men, Jin, Jay, Steve, and Phil. None of them were in the clinic but Jin had taken a previous lesson from me on the other side of the country.

They were all avid tennis players and have adapted quickly to the game of pickleball and recently started playing in some tournaments.

"Good morning, guys. How are ya today?" I ask.

I get a variety of grunts, groans, and one enthusiastic, "Grrrreat!"

"Alright," I say. "So, why are we here? What can I help you with?"

Jin starts off, "Last time we worked together, Prem, you really helped me with my soft game and it's going great. But when I'm playing against people who are into the wham-bam game, it's hard for me to slow the ball down and take control of the point."

"Gotcha," I say. "And...You, gentlemen?"

"I have quick reflexes," says Steve, "so I can react to a lot of shots, but I think I'd be even better off if I could learn to anticipate shots better. I know a little bit from my tennis experience but there must be ways to read a person's shot earlier than I do now."

"That's right," I answer, "there are, and we can definitely go over some of those today… Jay? Phil? How about you?"

Jay answers, "Well, I've got a gal I've been playing with in quite a few tournaments, and of course, they hit almost all the balls to her. I've tried poaching a couple times but I usually either hit it into the net or leave the court wide open, so I'd like a couple pointers for how to handle that situation, both in tournament play and recreationally."

"Yeah," Phil says, "all that sounds good, and on the same note, I feel like there's more I could be doing to get on the same page strategy-wise with my partner during a tournament. I end up with someone new every time I play and it never feels very cohesive."

"Alright," I say, "sounds great. I'm looking forward to all these topics. Let's start with Phil's question about partner communication during a tournament, since I think we can cover that pretty quickly."

At the lower levels, my private lessons are almost all drilling, but at the more advanced levels, we will often get into a longer discussion regarding strategy before doing drills.

Pre-Game Partner Communication

Tell Them Your Weakness

"If you get a chance to practice with your partner before a tournament, be sure to let them know what you're working on. Specifically, tell them what areas of your game you are trying to improve, and how that impacts them."

"But Prem," Jin asks, "what if we end up playing them later in a different event? Aren't we giving away our weaknesses?"

"Giving them this information will help you become a better player faster, <u>*especially*</u> if they then decide to use it against you. Remember, the goal is for you to *become a better pickleball player*, NOT to just keep beating the same people you always beat.

"Here are some examples of what you might say to a new partner:

- *I have a tendency to creep in on your forehand, but don't let me!! You go ahead and take those balls (or even better, call them 'Mine!') just to make sure I let you have it.*
- *I have noticed that I keep backing up from the kitchen line lately. If you notice me dropping back, will you please remind me to come up, either during or after the point?*
- *I am trying to develop my soft game, but I always seem to get suckered into slamming the ball. If you can, please just say, 'Slow...' during or after the point to remind me."*

Point Out Your Opponent's Weakness

"Another thing that's super-important to do at the beginning of a game is to point out your opponent's weakness if you see it.

Is one (or both) of your opponents left-handed? Do you know from prior experience that they have a tendency to hit shots down the line? Or, they love to lob?

"Share this info with your partner so she or he knows what to expect. Also share this kind of information between points, as each of you notice new patterns in your opponents' play. No offense to my wife, but it's always amazing to me how oblivious she is to the things that seem obvious to me on the court. It's my job, since I see them, to share the intel with her, so to speak."

Now, the next tip, which is very important for tournament play, will lead into Jay's question about poaching.

Decide Who You're Hitting To (Essential for Tournament Play, Optional for Recreational)

"For a number of reasons, your team should pick one person to hit eighty percent of your shots to, and it's important to communicate beforehand about which player that is going to be.

"At the Open tournament level, targeting one person is a common (and usually very effective) strategy for all doubles events, and is ESPECIALLY seen at the higher levels of mixed doubles, where the female is (generally correctly) presumed to be the weaker player (if only due to strength and power differences).

"At lower levels of mixed doubles, it can be a mixed bag. Due to the fact that success in this game we love is very much a matter of patience and finesse, it's not safe to always assume that the woman is necessarily the weaker player.

"In addition to keeping the ball away from the stronger player, targeting one person increases the likelihood they will make an error because that person may not have time to get ready between shots and it can be intimidating when they feel like all the pressure is on them.

"Plus, when you and your partner can anticipate which side of the court you're both hitting to, it makes it easier to stay in the right position. If you're not sure who is weaker or they seem to be at about the same level, just pick one person for a few points and if it isn't effective, try hitting to the other one.

"At the recreational level, it's just plain annoying when this happens to you because it's like a game of two-on-one and you spend most of your time on the court watching the ball go by.

"But there *are* ways to practice this strategy without mind-numbing your opponents. Alternate which player you hit to every few points or based on the score. When you're winning, hit to the stronger player. When the score is tied or if you're behind, hit to the weaker player."

(Do I need to remind you again that the goal is for you to become a better pickleball player, not to just keep beating the same people you always beat?)

Tips for Poaching: What to Do When Your Partner's Getting ALL The Balls

"Now, let's get back to Jay's question about poaching."

In case you're not familiar with the term, poaching is what happens when one person moves out of position to take shots that would otherwise be their partner's shot to play. It's what you might consider doing when your partner's the one they are targeting.

"The main reasons to poach are in the hopes of:

1. Finishing the Point

2. Catching Your Opponents Off-Guard

3. Give Some Relief to Your Partner When They're Being Targeted.

4. "The first tip I have for you, which is very simple, is to ask your partner's permission to poach."

1. Ask Your Partner's Permission First

"This should be a no-brainer, but unfortunately it's not. If you're playing recreationally, asking is just the courteous thing to do. You could say, 'Hey, do you mind if I take some of your balls if I can get them?' Some people will say, 'Heck, No! Please! Go ahead and help me!' Others, will give you an icy glare followed by a, 'Thanks, but I'd like to get my own balls.' (Imagine the scorn, the eye-rolls, and the complaining after the game if you *hadn't* asked!)

"In tournament play, it is even more important to ask your partner if they mind if you poach so that you foster a sense of really working as a team (and decrease the likelihood of building dissension).

"If you poach without asking and (heaven forbid) you miss the shot, you will likely hear a sigh of frustration and a mumbled, 'I would have had that shot!' *(And, if that happens, and your partner also happens to be your SPOUSE, I really wish you the grace of God!)*"

"Once you have permission to poach, it's more likely that, even if you miss a shot, your partner will perceive it as you trying to back them up rather than you trying to steal their shot.

"So always ask first."

2. Poach When Your Opponents Are Being Predictable but Don't Be Predictable When You Poach

"If your opponents haven't established a set pattern, don't try poaching because chances are it will only move you out of position and they will easily take advantage of the empty court you leave behind you. (This is the reason you see less poaching in the higher men's and women's doubles, because players are looking for that opening and ready to take advantage of it.) It's even worse if you're *predictably* poaching because then your opponents are just waiting for the open court.

"Instead, wait until there are several points where they have consistently hit to your partner, look for the pattern, and poach only when you are pretty confident that you know where the ball is going *before your opponent even hits it."*

3. Only Try to Poach When Your Forehand Is in the Middle

"Not only is the forehand the stronger shot for most players, it also allows you the greatest reach without moving too far out of position. So if you're a righty, focus on poaching when you are on the odd (left) side of the court, and if you're a lefty, poach when you're on the even (right) side of the court."

4. Have Your Partner Hit Toward the Middle

"When your partner gets in a tight cross-court dinking rally or a head-to-head volley you can't do much more than just stand back and watch. Instead, ask your partner to hit balls toward the middle. This cuts off the angles your opponents can play and makes it easier for you to step in and take a ball, hopefully catching your opponents by surprise, or at the very least giving your partner a few extra seconds to regroup and prepare for the next shot. This is a very important time to *call the ball*."

5. Get a Better Partner

"Now, I mean this in the nicest way possible. (If it were even possible to say something like that nicely....)

"If you really want to improve your game, find a partner who is better than you so that YOU are considered the weaker player and receive most of the balls. This will go SO much further toward improving your game than learning how to poach better.

"Does all that make sense?" I ask the group.

"Yep, all good stuff," Jay says. "I look forward to practicing, but before we start hitting the ball, do you have any tips for how to better anticipate our opponent's shots? I'm not sure whether it's best to watch the ball, the paddle, or the position of their body."

"Absolutely," I answer. "I like to call it learning how to predict the future."

Jay laughs. "Yeah, that'd be nice!"

When receiving a shot from my opponent, should I be watching the ball, the position of their paddle, or the position of their shoulders?

"Some players and coaches will tell you to watch the paddle for where they are going to hit the ball. However, I find that that doesn't give you much of a heads-up as to where the ball is going, because you don't know where the paddle is going to be facing until they are about to hit the ball.

"There are really only two options when trying to keep track of the ball AND the shoulder.

"One, you can develop your peripheral vision such that, while you keep your eye on the ball, you can still take in information about your opponent's body position. My wife, Wendy, swears that this is what I do, but it's not easy to do, much less teach.

"Or, two, watch the ball when it is coming in your direction but look at your opponent's shoulder/positioning when the ball is headed toward them, i.e. after you or your partner have hit the ball.

"One thing I hear over and over is how 'relaxed' I look on the court. Sure, part of it is just my personality—and a good ability to *look* like I don't have the butterflies, even when I *do*. But another important factor is that, most of the time, I have anticipated my opponent's hit two, or even three shots ahead, rather than simply reacting to the shot they just hit.

Think about it: If you don't know where your opponent's ball is going until AFTER they hit it, you've only got milliseconds to react and respond.

"If you don't know where your opponent's ball is going until AFTER they hit it, you've only got milliseconds to react and respond. Whereas, the further in advance you know (or can make a strong prediction) about what direction they are going to hit the ball, the more time you have to prepare, get in position, and plan YOUR next shot.

"My hope is to give you at least an extra second of time to prepare for your shot.

"For beginning players as well as experienced tournament players, having even just this short amount of extra time is likely to have your opponents ooh-ing and ahh-ing over your 'quick response times' when, secretly, you know that you were getting ready before they even hit their shot.

"Here is my best tip for how to 'see into the future' and predict your opponent's shot..."

Look at Their Leading Shoulder

"There are other parts of the body (such as the foot and the wrist) that provide a 'tell' as to where the ball is going to go, however for the majority of players, the majority of the time, the only thing you need to pay attention to is where their leading shoulder is pointing, and that will tell you where the ball is going."

What Is a "Leading Shoulder"?

"The leading shoulder is the shoulder on the opposite side of where they are hitting the ball. For right-handed players, the leading shoulder on a forehand is their left shoulder. On the backhand, it's their right shoulder.

"For left-handed players, the leading shoulder is their right shoulder on a forehand and the left shoulder on the backhand."

What Does the Leading Shoulder Tell You?

"The leading shoulder pretty much tells you exactly which direction they are going to hit the ball. Wherever that shoulder is pointing is where the ball is most likely going to go."

If the Leading Shoulder is pointing left, get ready for the ball to come to your left side. If it's pointing right, get ready for a ball at your right.

"(Even if many good players couldn't consciously tell you that this is how they know where the ball is going, they probably pick up on it subconsciously.)"

In the photo above, the most likely shot that I would hit would go to the near left side of the court. Do you see why?

Why Is This So?

"It has to do with the mechanics of the arm and shoulder. Once you are in position and your shoulder is planted, that's virtually the only shot you can hit if your wrist is firm and in line with your forearm."

Does This Really Apply to EVERYONE?

"This is true for the majority of players, the majority of the time. Chances are that anyone who is coming from a tennis, baseball, golf, football, volleyball, or basketball background is going to keep their wrist firm at the point of impact and their shoulder positioning will be a perfectly reliable indicator.

"The smaller percentage of pickleball players who come from a table tennis, badminton, racketball, squash, or cricket background are the ones who are more likely to be able to disguise their shots by throwing in a wrist movement at the point of contact.

"But again, that is for a *minority* of their shots. Looking at their shoulder should still give you a heads-up on the majority of their shots.

"It's worth sacrificing a point or two (or heck, a whole game!) for the sake of paying extra close attention to your opponent's leading shoulder and then seeing for yourself how that predicts where their shot is going to go."

Move Left or Right Before They Even Hit the Ball

"Now, this is also particularly helpful when you are preparing a defensive shot. Let's say you or your partner hit a really bad drop shot or lob and one of your opponents is lining up to hit an overhead. (Not that that scenario would *ever* actually happen to you. This is *just* a hypothetical, riiiiiight?)"

"When a right-handed person hits an overhead, it is nearly always going to go in front of them, or to THEIR left side because of the mechanics of the hips, shoulder and elbow. Only very 'wristy' players will hit an 'inside out' shot, where the ball flies off their paddle to their right. When you're playing against one of the few of them (or should I say us?), you'll have to take that into account, but for the vast majority of players you'll find yourself across the net from, you can bet that when they slam the ball, it's gonna go to the middle of your court, or to your RIGHT.

"When a right-handed opponent is on the 'even' side of the court, he or she will most likely hit the ball to the center or to the sideline on your right, so it's best for you and your partner to shift your positioning to the right, so that the person on the odd court is near the centerline and the person on the even court is near the right-hand sideline.

"When a right-handed opponent is on the "odd" side of the court, they tend to rotate their body open to the right in order to get a better aim at the court, so they will most often hit toward the center of the court, but occasionally toward your left, so it's best for you and your partner to shift your positioning to the left, so that the person on the odd court is near the left-hand sideline and the person on the even court is near the center line.

"This will give you the best chance of being in the right position to be able to return the slam.

"Of course, there are going to be times when there's nothing you can do but mutter under your breath and wince as the ball gets pounded at your feet. But for the rest of the times, I hope that this section has given you some new strategies to implement the next time you or your partner hits a bad shot. Remember, it's not over 'til it's over, so stay in the game, anticipate your opponent's shot, and try to stay in the point.

"Once you get used to reading these valuable clues, you too, will be able to predict the future," I say, only slightly ironically.

"Okay, let's get back to Jin's question about how to slow the ball down. First I'm going to show you how I do it and then we'll discuss what exactly I'm doing. Jay, you can smack the ball pretty good when you want to. Would you come over here to demonstrate so Jin can watch?"

Jay and I both stand at the kitchen line on either side of the net. I instruct him to slam every ball he can at me.

Shot after shot, I block the ball so it drops pretty gently into the kitchen on the other side of the net.

After about fifteen or twenty balls, I pause and look at the group.

"Yes!" Jin exclaims, "Exactly! That's what I want to learn how to do!"

"Okay," I say. "So what did you notice?"

"Well, you took all the pace off the ball," Jin answers.

"And you're not hitting it, you're just blocking it," Steve says.

"Okay, what else did you notice?" I ask.

"You're not backing up from the line," Phil responds.

"Yep," I say. "And what else?"

"Well, you always have your paddle up, but when you hit these shots, your paddle is parallel to the net instead of perpendicular," Jin adds.

"Definitely," I answer. "Those are all valid observations, but what exactly did you see me do, which allows the ball to slow down? Let's give them one more demonstration, Jay."

Smash. Block. And the ball drops into the kitchen.

Smash. Block. Drop.

Smash. Block. Drop.

Smash. Block. Drop.

"Oh, I see!" Jin calls out, excitedly. "You're bringing your paddle in toward you at the moment of contact!"

"You got it," I say. "And actually, I'm not sure if you can tell, but I also loosen my grip on the paddle. Both of those changes are what absorb the momentum of the ball. Now we're gonna do a couple more and I want you to pay attention to the direction of the face of my paddle."

Smash. Block. Drop.

Smash. Block. Drop.

Phil says, "As you hit every shot, the face of your paddle is facing downward toward your opponent's feet."

"Exactly," I answer. "Those are the three most important pieces. Loosen your grip, pull the paddle back at the moment of contact, and direct it downward so the ball doesn't pop back up where your opponents can smash it."

"Wow, I can really see how those things can make a difference, Prem," Steve says. "But again, you seem to have your paddle in the modified ready position before they even hit the ball. How do you know when they're going to smack it?"

"Aaah," I answer, "that's where I look for the wind-up. In order to hit the ball hard, your opponent has to get more backswing than usual to get the power, so when you see your opponent winding up, you know that it's time to get ready to block. Make sense?"

They all nod.

"Now, pair up and let's see you practice some."

When You See the Wind-Up, Get Your Paddle Parallel to the Net and Up in Front of Your Chest

At the Moment of Impact, Loosen Your Grip, Bring the Paddle Toward You, and Face It Slightly Downward

We do that thing that I do in my private lessons. They do a lot of drilling, I keep offering feedback and tweaks to help them get the results they want, and by the time our ninety minutes are up, I can tell these guys are thrilled with the progress they've made.

"Prem, it's been a pleasure. This was really great. I can't wait to schedule a lesson with you next time you're in town," Jin says.

"Yes! Me, too," Steve chimes in.

"You know, I coached tennis for years, Prem, and I can honestly say you've got a gift. Thanks so much for your help today," Phil adds.

"Definitely," Jay says.

"Thanks so much, guys, it was my pleasure," I answer, as I wave goodbye. Next, I gather my water bottle, ball hopper, and paddles, and meander back to what my daughter calls "The Pickleball Guru car" (because of the magnets on the side).

I'm pleasantly worn out, but filled up with the knowledge of how satisfied my students are, how much I love what I do, and the fact that *this* is what I (get to) do to support my family.

Onward & Upward

Well, we've been on quite the journey together through this book. You've gotten *more* information than my students would usually get, condensed into a *shorter* amount of time, *without* any practice or drilling built in along the way.

So what's next?

How do you process it all?

What can you do to integrate this information into your game?

The answer is: practice, practice, practice.

Pickleball Is No Different from Any Other Sport

You see, it's taken for granted in every other sport that you have to drill and practice to improve. That's why there are driving ranges in golf. That's why there are batting cages in baseball. And that's why there are ball machines in tennis.

Back in my days of playing world-class table tennis, I regularly hit backhands for a solid two to three hours, and *then* I hit forehands for at least another two hours.

Only in pickleball is it still often taken for granted that we can get better just by going out and playing our everyday games.

It simply isn't true.

I first met one of the top players in the country, Wes Gabrielsen, when I played against him (and beat him) in a tournament a few years ago.

Being an excellent tennis player, he had a lot of raw talent but hadn't yet mastered the finer points of pickleball. Fast-forward two years and he won three gold medals in the national tournament. Many people asked him how he had improved so quickly and his standard answer was, "Hours of drills." (I'm pretty sure my days of beating him in tournaments are over.)

If even someone with so much prior experience and so much natural talent had to drill to get better, I can promise you the rest of us need practice, too.

It's simply too hard to make a dramatic improvement during real play, ESPECIALLY if you're playing against the same or lower level players. It's too easy to get taken over by the drive to win a point and you forget anything you've previously learned.

Yet, how often do you yowl in frustration when you hit a ball out? (No offense, but how many times in your life have you actually PRACTICED that shot you just missed? Probably not very many...)

If You Want to Get Better, Drill. If You Don't, Don't.

Now, I know that there are a few of you who DO drill on a regular basis. And I know that there are others of you who would LIKE to, but don't have a bucket of balls, or a partner to hit with.

But the vast majority of players, especially those who are amongst the better players in their local group, never hit a shot outside the context of a game.

But if you actually want to become a better player, it means doing some drills. If you're committed to improving your level of play, it means going over the basics. And if you want to win more games, it means reducing your unforced errors so that you aren't just GIVING away points.

It Doesn't Hurt to Practice Anything – and Everything!

Now some people, particularly those in the 4.0-5.0 levels, tend to think it's beneath them when they see that in Level 1 of The Pickleball Guru Academy, we cover Serves, Return of Serves, and Drop Shots. They think to themselves, *Duh, I already know how to serve and return the serve, why not just focus on the drop shot?* And when they see that Level 2 covers the Dink, Volley, and Put-Away Shots, they either think *Ugggh, dinking is for wimps, I hate to dink!* or they *know* they need to practice the dink, but they think they have the volley and put-aways down.

Well, let me ask, when was the last time you missed a dink? Or a volley? Or a put-away? Or a serve? Or a return of serve? Of course, most of us miss at least one of them, almost every time we're out on the court.

No matter your skill level, if you truly want to improve your level of play, you'll benefit from drilling on the basics. EVERYONE will. We ALL need to strengthen our muscle memory on our good shots and we ALL need to reduce our unforced errors.

Have I drilled *that* into your head yet? ☺

How to Practice

To a certain extent, you can practice on your own. Better yet, get a partner and make it a weekly practice session. Even better, create a foursome dedicated to playing out practice points for a good half hour before starting to play for real.

I recently taught a series of clinics in Virginia. Afterwards the local USAPA Ambassador got a venue to give them extra court time exclusively for drilling. I wish every venue could have dedicated practice time like that.

If you are one of those "appliers" I mentioned earlier, you'll find a way to make time for practice. You're serious about improving your game and you'll find a partner, pick a time, and go drill. You're on the right track.

But if you're afraid that you're more likely to fall into the category of the "forgetters" here are a series of challenges you can complete as a means to begin integrating this into your level of play. For each challenge you may want to refer to the related drill mentioned in the book (use the Table of Contents for easy reference).

These challenges are designed to give you a singular focus for a period of recreational play. I recommend spending at least one day of practice on each challenge, but you might spend a week or more on each if you prefer. It all depends how frequently you play and how motivated you are to progress. You might be tempted to skip over the earlier challenges, but I encourage you to go through each in order. If you find that you struggle to complete one, then you know that that is an area where you should set aside some time to drill.

Personal Challenges for Recreational Play

Level 1

- ☐ **Challenge #1:** Ask a bystander to watch you play and call out "Paddle up!" anytime they see that your paddle is not out in front of your chest.
- ☐ **Challenge #2:** Focus on keeping your eye on the ball for the entire duration of every point and making a sound at the point of impact when you hit the ball.
- ☐ **Challenge #3:** Focus on hitting every serve deep and toward the middle of the court.
- ☐ **Challenge #4:** Focus on hitting every return of serve deep and toward the middle of the court.
- ☐ **Challenge #5:** Focus on calling every single ball either "You!" or "Me!" as soon as your opponent hits it.

Level 2

- ☐ **Challenge #6:** Focus on getting up to the net. As soon as you hit a return of serve, hurry up to the net. When you or your partner hits a successful drop shot, hurry up to the net.
- ☐ **Challenge #7:** Ask a bystander to stand near the net and tell you to "Get up!" if your feet are more than 6 inches from the kitchen line or to call "Foot fault!" if you volley the ball while touching the no-volley zone.
- ☐ **Challenge #8:** Focus on waiting until the ball almost bounces for the second time before hitting every shot today.
- ☐ **Challenge #9:** Focus on hitting every single ball toward the middle of the court.
- ☐ **Challenge #10:** Focus on hitting a controlled shot or dink for any ball that is below your shoulder level. Only hit a hard shot when you have an overhead shot and can put the ball away.

Level 3

- ☐ **Challenge #11:** Every time your team serves, attempt to hit the third shot of every point as a drop shot.
- ☐ **Challenge #12:** Focus on shifting left or right to cover the line or cover the middle. Move toward your sideline and mentally prepare to cover the line when the opponent opposite you is hitting the ball. Focus on moving slightly toward the middle and preparing to cover the middle when the opponent opposite your partner is hitting the ball.

- ☐ **Challenge #13:** Focus on politely getting in some games with better players.
- ☐ **Challenge #14:** Good-naturedly play at least two games with players who you tend to think of as "below your level." Use some of the mental games I mention earlier.
- ☐ **Challenge #15:** Focus on observing the correlation between your opponent's leading shoulder and the direction their shots go.

Bonus Level

- ☐ **Bonus Challenge #1:** Serve me an email at prem@thepickleballguru.com telling me what you've learned and applied from this book.
- ☐ **Bonus Challenge #2:** Ask your local USAPA ambassador to contact me to set up a clinic in your area.

Of course, one of the best places to practice what you'll read in this book is to join me for one of my highly acclaimed, frequently sold-out clinics, which I offer across the country throughout the year. (Or, better yet, invite me to your area to hold a clinic!) You can always find information about my upcoming clinics on my website at: www.ThePickleballGuru.com/schedule

Like all things in life, this book is in constant evolution. In 2015 I expect to launch levels three and four of The Pickleball Guru Academy. I will teach more, and learn even more *about* teaching. I look forward to offering you a revised edition or a companion to this book in the coming years.

In the meantime, I hope you've gotten a lot out of it. I encourage you to gift a copy to your partner, purchase a copy for your club's pickleball library, and reread it several times a year.

Wishing you all the best and happy pickling! I hope to see you out on the courts soon.

With warmest regards from your Smart Pickleball™ coach,

Prem

Prem Carnot
The Pickleball Guru

About the Author

Prem Carnot offers clinics and lessons across the country for pickleball players of all levels and especially for players of other racket sports who are new to the game.

For FREE monthly pickleball tips and to find out what strategy the National Champion used to make his highly skilled opponent look like a newbie (a strategy that you can use the next time you're out on the court), go to www.ThePickleballGuru.com/usa.

To inquire about scheduling a clinic in your neck of the woods, email prem@thepickleballguru.com.

56263421R00093

Made in the USA
Lexington, KY
17 October 2016